MIRACULOUS
IMAGES OF
OUR LORD

ST. CATHERINE DE RICCI (1522-1589) was a Dominican prioress and mystic who had frequent visions of the crucifixion of Christ. She received all the marks of His Passion, the five wounds and the crown of thorns. Our Lord once detached Himself from the crucifix in St. Catherine's cell to receive her loving embrace.

MIRACULOUS IMAGES OF OUR LORD

FAMOUS CATHOLIC STATUES, PORTRAITS AND CRUCIFIXES

By

Joan Carroll Cruz

"My heart hath said to thee: My face hath sought thee: thy face, O Lord, will I still seek. Turn not away thy face from me." —Psalms 26:8-9

TAN BOOKS AND PUBLISHERS, INC.
Rockford, Illinois 61105

OTHER BOOKS BY THE AUTHOR

Miraculous Images of Our Lady
Secular Saints
Prayers and Heavenly Promises
The Incorruptibles
Eucharistic Miracles
Relics
Desires of Thy Heart

Nihil Obstat: Rev. Stanley P. W. Klores
                   Censor Librorum

Imprimatur: ✠ Most Rev. Francis B. Schulte
                   Archbishop of New Orleans
                   July 14, 1993

The Nihil Obstat and Imprimatur are the Church's declarations that a work is free from error in matters of faith and morals. It in no way implies that the Church endorses the contents of the work.

Cover Picture: The San Damiano Crucifix, which spoke to St. Francis of Assisi.

Library of Congress Catalog Card No.: 93-61509

ISBN: 0-89555-496-8

Printed and bound in the United States of America.

TAN BOOKS AND PUBLISHERS, INC.
P.O. Box 424
Rockford, Illinois 61105
1995

"God does not work miracles and grant favors by means of some statues in order that these statues may be held in higher esteem than others, but that through His wonderful works He may awaken the dormant devotion and affection of the faithful."

—St. John of the Cross
Book III, Chapter 36, #1
Ascent of Mount Carmel

CONTENTS

vii

PART IV
OTHER MIRACULOUS IMAGES OF OUR LORD

AUTHOR'S NOTE

While researching the companion to this volume, *Miraculous Images of Our Lady,* it was a somewhat easy matter to find 100 images that were regarded as miraculous. There are many, many more images that could have been included in that volume, but it seemed best, in order not to have an overly large book, to stop at the round figure of 100.

For this volume, *Miraculous Images of Our Lord,* the gathering of miraculous images was not so easy. Despite diligent research, the present 42 images of our Saviour were all that this author could find. In the matter of miraculous images it would seem that Our Lord graciously concedes the greater portion of the privilege to our Holy Mother.

It was known to a number of Saints that many images of Our Blessed Mother and Our Lord were regarded as miraculous, and many were the saints who visited and prayed before these images. Some Saints have even acknowledged the miraculous nature of these images in their writings.

St. Louis De Montfort writes: "There is not a church without an altar in her [the Blessed Virgin Mary's] honor, not a country nor a canton where there are not some miraculous images where all sorts of evils are cured and all sorts of good gifts obtained."

St. Augustine, in writing about miraculous shrines, tells us that, ". . . it is seen and known by all men that God does set a difference between one place and another, though none can penetrate His counsel and explain why it is that miracles are wrought in one place and not in another."

St. Alphonsus Liguori writes, "The divine Mother has shown by prodigies how pleasing to her are the visits paid to her images. But if we are unable to visit her miraculous images which are far from home, we should visit her shrines which are readily available."

The Saint who has perhaps written the most regarding miraculous images is St. John of the Cross, who devoted Chapters 35-37 of Book III to this subject in his *Ascent of Mount Carmel.* The Saint first tells us,

ix

The Church established the use of statues for two principal reasons: the reverence given to the Saints, Our Lord and Our Lady through them; and the motivation of the will and the awakening of devotion to the Saints by their means. Insofar as they serve this purpose their use is profitable and necessary.

Again the Saint notes,

Experience even teaches that if God grants some favors and works miracles, He does so through some statues that are not very well carved or carefully painted, or that are poor representations, so that the faithful will not attribute any of these wonders to the statue or painting.

The miracles are attributed, of course, to the Heavenly Father, who works His wonders through the intercession of the heavenly person the image represents.

St. John of the Cross also writes,

I would like to mention some supernatural effects that certain images occasionally cause in particular individuals. God gives to some images a special spiritual influence upon souls so that their figure and the devotion they cause remain fixed in the mind as though they were present.

Images were not always favorably regarded. Early in the eighth century a heresy known as iconoclasm initiated an image-breaking campaign based on the theory that images, pictures and relics were idolatrous. The true Catholic attitude toward the veneration of images was clearly defined at the end of the period of iconoclasm by the Second Council of Nicaea in the year 787:

Images of Christ, and of His Mother and of other Saints are to be made and to be kept, and due honor and veneration is to be given them; not that any divinity or virtue is believed to be in them on account of which they would have to be honored, or that any prayer is to be addressed to them, or that any confidence is to be placed in them, as was formerly done by the heathens who placed their hopes in idols: but because the honor which is given them is referred to the originals which they represent; so that by kissing the images, by uncovering our heads or kneeling before them, we adore Christ and venerate His Saints, whose likeness they represent.

This teaching is still maintained by the Church.

It would be well to remember that these images would not be so reverently admired and elaborately enshrined in churches or religious houses if the phenomena associated with them had not been studied and approved by Church officials.

As a result of reading of the following marvels worked by God, may we grow ever more deeply in love with Our Lord and appreciate more fervently the pains He suffered for our redemption.

—Joan Carroll Cruz

DECLARATION OF OBEDIENCE

In obedience to the decrees of several Roman Pontiffs, in particular those of Pope Urban VIII, I declare that I in no way intend to prejudge Holy Mother the Church in the matter of miracles. Final authority in such matters rests with the Church, to whose judgment I willingly submit.

—Joan Carroll Cruz

MIRACULOUS
IMAGES OF
OUR LORD

—PART I—

MIRACULOUS IMAGES
OF THE CHILD JESUS

THE INFANT JESUS OF PRAGUE

Prague, The Republic of Czech
1556

While countless statues of the Christ Child are venerated only during the Christmas season, the statue of the Infant Jesus of Prague enjoys recognition throughout the year and experiences a worldwide reputation.

Although kept in the Republic of Czech (formerly Czechoslovakia), the statue is of Spanish origin and was given to a Spanish princess by her mother as a wedding gift. It was brought to Prague by the bride, Maria Manriques de Lara, after her marriage in 1556 to Vratislav of Pernstyn, a Czech nobleman. The statue once again served as a wedding gift when it was given to Maria's daughter, Polyxena, upon her marriage to Zdenek of Lobkovice. On being widowed in 1628, she decided to make the statue available to all believers by donating it to the Carmelites of Prague and the Church of Our Lady of Victory. Her words at the time proved prophetic: "I hereby give you what I prize most highly in this world. As long as you venerate this image you will not be in want." When special devotions were instituted in honor of the Child Jesus, the community, which had been enduring hardships, soon prospered.

The Child Jesus was particularly dear to one of the novices, Cyril of the Mother of God (1590-1675), who was delivered of interior trials by means of this devotion. The future history of the statue would in all probability have suffered if it had not been for this holy Carmelite.

At the beginning of the disturbances attending the Thirty Years' War, the novitiate was removed to Germany in 1630. With the absence of the novices and Brother Cyril, devotions before the statue were gradually neglected until the prayers were abandoned altogether. Need and distress once more returned. Eventually the invading army of King Gustavus Adolphus of Sweden took possession of the churches in the city, plundered the Carmelite monastery and threw the image of the Infant Jesus onto a heap of rubble behind the high altar. For the next seven years the statue lay forgotten by all. On the feast of Pentecost in 1637, Cyril of the Mother of God, now an ordained priest, returned to Prague. Because hostile armies still overran the city, the community was in distress until Fr. Cyril remembered the prosperity and peace they had enjoyed while devotions to the Infant Jesus were observed. He searched for the lost statue and eventually found it almost buried in dust and debris. Made of wood and coated with wax, the image had miraculously suffered little from its neglect, except the statue's two hands were missing. Cyril placed the statue atop an altar in the oratory and reorganized devotions to it. One day, while praying before the statue, he distinctly heard these words: "Have pity on Me, and I will have pity on you. Give Me My hands, and I will give you peace. The more you honor Me, the more I will bless you."

When money intended for the repair of the statue was spent on a replacement, the Infant manifested His displeasure by causing the new statue to be shattered by a falling candlestick. Once again the original statue became the object of veneration, but when additional funds for the necessary repairs proved to be slow in coming, Fr. Cyril again heard the voice: "Place Me near the entrance of the sacristy, and you will receive aid." When this was done, the full cost of the repairs was promptly donated.

The needs of the community were always met through the continued devotion to the Child Jesus, and such were the favors granted that replicas of the statue were made for those who likewise wanted to benefit from the generous favors of the holy Child.

It became the traditional practice of the shrine in Prague to clothe the statue several times each year in the proper liturgical color. The most beautiful garment in the collection is an ermine cloak placed on the statue the first Sunday after Easter, which is the anniversary day of the coronation of the statue by the bishop of Prague in 1655. During the Christmas season the statue is clothed in a dark green robe made of velvet and richly decorated with golden embroidery. This was a gift of the Empress Maria Theresa on the occasion of her coronation as queen of Bohemia in 1743. The Infant's wardrobe contains more than 50 dresses. Many, too, are the golden ornaments and chains, given by grateful devotees, which adorn the holy statue.

Since the time of the statue's ecclesiastical approbation in 1655, replicas always represent the royal status of the Child. Crowned and clothed in a mantle of fine fabrics, the statues hold in the left hand a sphere representing the world, while the right hand is raised in blessing.

Standing a mere 19 inches high, the statue is known throughout the world, with the word "miraculous" generally added to its title.

The original statue of the Infant Jesus is enshrined in a side chapel of the Church of Our Lady of Victory.

PRINCESS POLYXENA LOBKOWITZ donated the Infant of Prague statue to the Carmelites in Prague in 1628. She said, "I hereby give you what I prize most highly in this world. As long as you venerate this image you will not be in want."

THE INFANT JESUS OF PRAGUE, Czech Republic, was first venerated by Ven. Cyril of the Mother of God (1590-1675), pictured above. The holy Carmelite was delivered of interior trials by means of special devotions in honor of the Child Jesus.

THE MIRACULOUS STATUE of the Infant Jesus of Prague, ornately clothed in one of 50 specially crafted garments, is enshrined in Prague's Church of Our Lady of Victory.

CHINESE ROBES are worn by the Holy Infant in this photograph. The Child holds a sphere representing the world in the left hand, while raising the right hand in blessing.

ROYAL VESTMENTS, intricate in detail, here adorn the Infant Jesus of Prague. The statue, made of wood and coated with wax, stands only 19″ high.

THE MIRACULOUS STATUE appears at left without robes and at right clothed in a priestly alb, ready to be dressed in royal robes.

"THE LITTLE FLOWER," St. Thérèse of Lisieux, holding the hourglass, is pictured with a statue of the Infant of Prague. Such reproduction statues follow the design of the original statue, with the right hand raised in blessing.

THIS INFANT OF PRAGUE statue, a replica of the original statue of the Infant Jesus of Prague, was cared for in the cloister by St. Thérèse of the Child Jesus and the Holy Face.

THE INFANT JESUS OF PRAGUE

Arenzano, Liguria, Italy
1888

When the Discalced Carmelite friars decided in 1888 to build a monastery near Genoa, they selected the town of Arenzano, which is located by the Ligurian Sea. Twelve years later, Fr. Prior John of the Cross placed a picture of the Infant Jesus of Prague in their chapel. This simple little picture encouraged so much love and fervor for the Holy Child that devotion was well established by the time a replica of the Infant Jesus of Prague statue was donated by Marchioness Delfina Gavotti of Savona.

The statue was an exact replica of the Prague statue and was affectionately known as the "Great Little King." Robed in rich garments, it was solemnly blessed on June 15, 1902. The generosity of the Infant's devotees was such that construction on a larger church was begun with the funds received from grateful recipients of His favors. This church, whose cornerstone was laid in 1904, is regarded as the first church in the world to be dedicated to the Infant Jesus of Prague.

By 1918 the belfry was completed which was to house four bells of varying sizes. The largest bell was blessed and dedicated to the Infant Jesus. On it was embossed: "Carmelite Fathers dedicated me to the Child Jesus of Prague, that with my voice I would proclaim His glory; that all would know and worship the Divine Child Jesus, God and Man; that He would rain on them His graces."

For the solemn coronation of the statue, Pope Pius XI presented a crown of gold which was embellished with brilliants and small diamonds. Fashioned in Geneva by the goldsmith Mr. Dodevilla, the crown was taken to Rome and blessed by the holy Pontiff. The coronation ceremony, performed by the Vatican's Secretary of State, Rafael Cardinal Merry del Val, took place on Sept. 6, 1924. Four years later the Church of the Infant of Prague was raised to the dignity of a minor basilica.

After Italy surrendered to the Allies and the United States in 1944, the Nazis began bombing cities near Arenzano. The citizens of the city turned to the Infant Jesus for protection and promised to provide His statue with a golden orb for His left hand if all the citizens were spared.

During five days of utter terror in August of 1944, bombs continued to fall upon the city, destroying homes and a small parish church. When the bombing stopped four bodies were found, but these were identified as strangers who were apparently passing through the town when the bombing commenced.

Since all the citizens of Arenzano survived, the Holy Infant had proved His power of protection. In gratitude, a golden orb was ceremoniously placed in the hand of their little Benefactor.

The large number of the Infant's devotees inspired the formation of the Confraternity of the Infant Jesus of Prague. Approved by the Archbishop, Monsignor Edward Pulciano, on October 13, 1903, it was highly enriched with indulgences by Pope Pius X. Those wanting to join this pious union should write to Rev. Fr. Prior, O.D.C., 16011 Arenzano (Genoa) Italy.

THE "GREAT LITTLE KING" statue, a replica of the original image, was solemnly crowned in Arenzano, Italy, by Pope Pius XI in 1924. A golden orb was placed in the Holy Infant's hand in 1944 in appreciation for protection against Nazi bombing.

THE HOLY INFANT OF GOOD HEALTH

Morelia, Michoacan, Mexico
1942

One day, an unknown woman was going from door to door in the city of Morelia trying to sell a small statue of the Infant Jesus. When she stopped at a particular house, the woman who answered the door remembered that her godchild, now a grown woman, had wanted such a statue from her earliest childhood. The purchase was made, but the godmother, acting on an interior impulse, decided to keep the statue secret until such time as her godchild, who was then living in Mexico City, would return permanently to Morelia.

Measuring a mere 11 inches in height, the statue had been carved by a skillful hand of fine-grained, fragrant wood and was beautiful in all respects. Delighted with her purchase, the godmother was anxious to present her godchild with the statue. However, each time the young lady returned to Morelia for a visit, she expressed no desire to return permanently to her native city. After each visit the godmother was disappointed that she could not present the young lady with the statue, and she never told her godchild of the surprise that awaited her permanent return.

Then one day, much to the surprise of the family, the young lady announced that she had decided to live in Morelia for the rest of her life. The godmother, delighted with the news, happily presented the statue to her godchild. As soon as the statue came into the possession of the young lady, the Holy Infant began to work what appeared to be extraordinary cures in favor of the sick who prayed before the Infant. After witnessing a number of these cures, the owner decided to address her wonder-working statue as "The Holy Infant of Good Health," a title that all considered appropriate.

One of the earliest devotees of the little statue was a physician who, together with the owner, organized the first public demonstration that took place on April 21, 1944 in the Capuchin church.

During the service the statue was given a small crown that had been donated by a woman physician. After this ceremony, it became the custom to honor the Holy Infant each April 21 with a Holy Mass offered at one of the churches in the city.

The cures worked by Our Lord through this likeness became known throughout Mexico and especially in Mexico City, where a Poor Clare nun composed a novena in the Infant's honor. Approved by His Excellency, Luis Maria Altamirano y Bulnes on December 5, 1946, it was made public for the first time in the Church of Our Lady of Mercy in Morelia.

The Archbishop of Morelia suggested in 1957 that the statue be removed from the house of the owner and placed in a church, where the Infant Jesus would be more accessible to His devotees. With a heavy heart the owner gave her consent. Great pomp and ceremony accompanied the Holy Infant of Good Health as it was taken from the owner's home and carried to the Church of Our Lady of Mt. Carmel in Morelia. This took place on December 15, 1957. Witnessing this transfer were the Archbishop of Morelia, various ecclesiastics, many priests and nuns representing the many religious orders of Mexico and the United States, as well as distinguished laymen. During the impressive ceremony that followed the transfer, the Archbishop of Morelia blessed the statue and its golden crown.

It soon became obvious that the Holy Infant should have His own church in Morelia. A campaign to collect monies for this project was soon organized, a distinguished architect was selected and land was purchased. The cornerstone for this new church was laid in 1958; the consecration of the completed church took place in 1963.

The miracles worked by the Holy Infant of Good Health are numerous, and in most cases were described and verified by physicians. One of the doctors, Antonio Marin Landa, tells that he placed his whole family under the protection of the Holy Child and writes, "Of His immeasurable greatness He has lavished many miracles on me in the past, and I am still experiencing them today, as I hope to go on experiencing them in the future, out of the treasures of His inexhaustible goodness."

The doctor goes on to tell of his preservation from injury after the bus in which he was riding fell off a precipice, of his son who was preserved from serious injury after being gored in the chest by a bull, and the safety of his brother, who escaped his house as it was being destroyed in a sudden and terrible flood.

One of the most remarkable cures involved a four-year-old boy who had sustained a shock that left him deaf, dumb and paralyzed. His case was pronounced hopeless. On learning of the Holy Infant, the boy's parents carried him to the home of the statue's owner and recited prayers before the holy image. A month later, when the child remained in the same condition, the family began a novena to the Holy Infant. As part of the novena they carried the child each day to the statue. On the sixth day of the novena the boy started to move; on the seventh day he started to talk; on the eighth day he began to walk and on the ninth day he was completely cured.

In addition to the preservation of life in desperate situations, the Holy Infant of Good Health has cured cases of infantile paralysis, heart ailments, brain injuries, severe tonsilitis, infections, rare fevers and many other ailments.

Wearing a decorated dress and elaborate cape, the Infant holds a golden scepter in His left hand while raising a graceful right hand in blessing. The Holy Infant of Good Health awaits the visits of His needy clients in the splendid church in Morelia that bears His name.

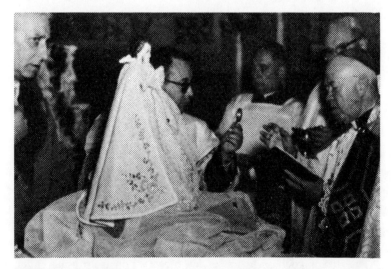

OFFICIAL BLESSING. The Archbishop of Morelia, Mexico, is pictured in 1957 blessing the statue of the Holy Infant.

Photo: McGrew, K.C., Mo

THE HOLY INFANT OF GOOD HEALTH, Morelia, Mexico, has worked numerous miracles, including the preservation of life in precarious situations, as well as curing heart ailments, brain injuries and many other ailments.

A GOLDEN SCEPTER in His left hand, the Holy Infant of Good Health raises a graceful right hand in blessing.

THE HOLY CHILD OF ATOCHA

Atocha, Madrid, Spain
and
Plateros, Zacatecas, Mexico

While the Moors were ravaging Spain, there existed in the town of Atocha a statue of the Blessed Mother and the Child Jesus that was dear to the hearts of the people. It was a unique image in that the Child Jesus, which rested on the arm of His Mother, was not attached to the figure of the Blessed Virgin, but was a separate statue. Because of this separation, the image of the Child was often brought to the homes of the sick or dying. It was especially cherished by expectant mothers who requested that the image be brought to their bedsides during their deliveries. It provided not only encouragement to the mothers during their labors, but it was also thought that the Holy Child gave a special blessing to the babies at the moment of birth and that the newborns would thereafter be under His protection. Because of its many travels, the statue was appropriately clothed in garments resembling those of a pilgrim.

A legendary account tells that the statue became known for another area of activity during a certain time of the Moorish occupation, when the heads of households and other men were imprisoned. Contact with the men was expressly forbidden, except for children under the age of 12 who were allowed to bring food to the members of their families. The prisoners who had no children were destined to starve, since the Moors refused to provide food for them. But the prisoners did not starve. They prayed for relief and were soon visited by a mysterious child, described as beautiful and unearthly, who made the rounds each night bringing food and water. The child was dressed as a pilgrim. In one hand he held a basket filled with bread; the other hand held a pilgrim staff that supported a gourd of water. The prisoners soon noticed that the basket was always filled with bread and the gourd was always filled with water, no matter how many men benefitted from his ministry.

19

After a time, the identity of the child was suspected when it was noticed that the rope sandals on the statue of the Child Jesus in the church were soiled and worn. Replaced with new sandals, these again became soiled and worn. It is not known how long these visitations took place.

It is sad to report that representatives of the Basilica de Nuestra Señora de Atocha tell that the statue of the Little Pilgrim was lost long ago under circumstances that are unknown. Although official logs detailing the miracles attributed to the Child of Atocha did not survive, some of the Little Pilgrim's miracles were given by the Spanish writer Alfonso el Sabio in his *Cantigas*. Other documents, as well, speak of the miracles worked by the Holy Child during the Moorish occupation.

Existing in Atocha at the same time was another statue of Mother and Child. After the loss of the Little Pilgrim, the attention of the people was directed to this image, which captured the love and devotion that the former statue had enjoyed. Known as Our Lady of Atocha, it has been revered by the people of the area for many centuries. Unlike the statue that was lost, the figures of this Mother and Child were carved from the same block of wood. The Child Jesus is not separated from His Mother and is, therefore, not removable.

According to legend, the statue was carved by Nicodemus, painted by the Apostle St. Luke and brought by some of St. Peter's disciples to Spain, where it found its way to the town of Atocha. According to several nineteenth-century experts, the statue belongs to the Byzantine school and was carved before the time of the Crusades. A similarity is noted between this statue and another Spanish statue known as Our Lady of Montserrat, which dates from the eighth century. Our Lady of Atocha is different in that she holds in her right hand an apple which is thought to represent the apple of our first parents. Our Lady of Montserrat holds a sphere representing the earth.

The memory of the Little Pilgrim was brought to the New World when Spanish missionaries immigrated to Mexico with the Conquistadors during the sixteenth century. What attracted the Spaniards was the great amount of silver then being discovered in the state of Zacatecas. Under the supervision of Juan de Tolosa, the Conquistadors were rewarded with great wealth. They were also credited with founding the capital city, which was also called Zacatecas—an area that later witnessed a hard-fought battle in which the army of Pancho Villa defeated the forces of dictator Victoriano Huerta.

Near the capital is the mining city of Fresnillo. Four miles away is the town of Plateros, where a church was built in the mid sixteenth century that was dedicated to El Santo Cristo de los Plateros (The Holy Christ of the Silversmiths), whose history is given in another section of this book. In this church was placed a statue of the Blessed Mother which held a detachable image of the Holy Child. Donated around the year 1829, the statues were a gift of the Marques de San Miguel de Aguayo, a wealthy mine owner.

Because the Spaniards through the years had maintained the memory of the Holy Pilgrim, the immigrants brought with them a devotion to El Santo Niño de Atocha. It was not surprising then that the Spaniards who settled near, and in, Plateros would bestow the same name to this new statue of Mother and Child since the removable image of the Child Jesus reminded them of the Holy Pilgrim. Eventually the Holy Child was garbed as a little pilgrim with basket, gourd and pilgrim staff, but with a Mexican flair since the Holy Child wears a feathered, upturned hat that somewhat resembles a sombrero. The pilgrim costume of the Holy Child seems appropriate since He is often taken in processions, and frequently visits nearby churches.

Recalling the ministry of the Holy Pilgrim to the imprisoned in the Moorish jails, the people of Plateros placed under the protection of this new Holy Child all the workers who were "confined" in the mines.

The small figure is found in a niche of pink stone that is located above the main altar and just below the crucifix of the Holy Christ of the Silversmiths. In this niche the Holy Child is seated on a gilded chair that rests atop a dais. On special occasions, the Holy Child is returned to the arm of His Mother.

Devotion to the Holy Child of Atocha spread to the United States about the year 1831 and developed in this manner. Approximately 30 miles north of Santa Fe, New Mexico, was a ranch known as Potrero de Chimayo (Cattle ranch of Chimayo). The owner was Don Severiano Medina, who was in extreme pain and was almost paralyzed by arthritis. After learning of the miracles and the great devotion lavished upon the Holy Child of Atocha in Plateros, Mexico, he abandoned himself to the Holy Child's protection and was soon cured. In thanksgiving Don Severiano made the long, arduous journey to the shrine to offer his gratitude before the miraculous image. During his visit he purchased a small replica of the statue and carried it with him when he returned to New Mexico. As another expression of his gratitude, Don Severiano built a chapel on his ranch in Chimayo, where the little figure is still venerated.

Since that time replicas of the Holy Child have spread throughout the Southwest. During the various wars in which men from the area were engaged, the Holy Child's predecessor who had ministered to prisoners in Atocha, Spain was again remembered. When some of the men were being listed as prisoners of war, the people entrusted them to the care of the Holy Child of Atocha.

The Holy Child in Plateros has performed many miracles for his devotees, as evidenced by the countless retablos at the shrine in Mexico. Retablos are a type of ex-voto consisting of little pictures offered in thanksgiving for favors received. They either represent the Holy Child, or they depict the type of miracle credited to Him.

Devotion to the Holy Child of Atocha in Mexico, and in Southwest United States, is very vigorous, as was once the devotion given to the Holy Pilgrim, whose image was lost so long ago.

A REPLICA OF the little Pilgrim of Atocha, pictured here, is kept at the Discalced Carmelite monastery at Valladolid, Spain, which was founded by St. Teresa of Avila.

THE HOLY CHILD OF ATOCHA holds a bread basket in one hand; in the other hand rests a pilgrim staff that supports a gourd of water.

ATOCHA, SPAIN is also the home of this ancient statue of Mother and Child, known as Our Lady of Atocha.

REVERED FOR CENTURIES, this Spanish statue of Our Lady of Atocha is thought by some to have been carved by Nicodemus, painted by St. Luke and carried to Spain by disciples of St. Peter. The image of Our Lady holds an apple, perhaps to represent the apple of Adam and Eve. The Christ Child is not removable, as with other versions of the image.

SPANIARDS WHO SETTLED in the area of Plateros, Mexico were very pleased with the statue pictured above because it reminded them of the Christ Child of Atocha, Spain. This statue was constructed so that the image of the Child can be removed from the arm of the Mother.

THE PILGRIM COSTUME of the Holy Child of Atocha statue of Plateros, Zacatecas, Mexico is appropriate since the statue is often taken in procession and frequently visits nearby churches.

ON DISPLAY, the Holy Child of Atocha of Mexico is seated on a gilded chair in a niche on the altar near the crucifix of the Holy Christ of the Silversmiths (see Chapter 15).

THE BASKET, PILGRIM'S HAT and staff are familiar symbols of the Christ Child of Atocha. Note the shell on His cloak; the wearing of shells on clothing or hats originated at the shrine of St. James at Compostella, Spain. They were given at the end of a pilgrimage as proof that the long journey had been completed.

— 5 —

THE HOLY INFANT OF CEBU

Cebu, The Philippines
1521

Located between the South China Sea and the Pacific Ocean, the Republic of The Philippines is found off the southeast coast of Asia and consists of thousands of islands. One of these is the island of Cebu, which was the first Philippine island to be Christianized and the first to be blessed with a Catholic church. It is also at Cebu that the miraculous statue of the Infant Jesus is enshrined.

The history of the Holy Infant dates back to the discovery of the islands by Ferdinand Magellan, a native of Portugal who sailed for the interests of Spain. This explorer discovered the Philippines on March 16, 1521. After the chieftain, Rajah Humabon, permitted the seamen to land, Magellan immediately began to propagate the Catholic Faith. His efforts were met with immediate success, as indicated by the hundreds of natives who received the Sacrament of Baptism exactly one week after Magellan's arrival. Among these converts were Rajah Humabon and his wife. To this first Christian queen of Cebu, Magellan gave a gift: a carved wooden image of the Child Jesus.

Unfortunately, the good will of the converts began to deteriorate when Magellan tried to force a recognition of Rajah Humabon as the Christian leader of all the chiefs of Cebu, and perhaps of all the chiefs in the Philippine Islands. During a battle between the followers of Rajah Humabon and the natives of Mactan, Magellan was met with hostile refusal which led to his tragic death on the Island of Mactan on April 27, 1521, six weeks after his arrival in the Philippines.

Some days later, Rajah Humabon had an elaborate meal prepared for the seamen who were scheduled to depart for Spain. The plan was a sinister one, since the unsuspecting diners were poisoned. Those who survived fled for refuge to the Moluccas and then sailed for Spain.

30

It has been surmised that after Magellan's defeat, the image of the Infant Jesus that had been given to the chieftain's wife at her Baptism was relegated to the role of a pagan idol or an image of little value. It is perhaps for this reason that legend tells of the image being given to children to play with as a toy.

The legend continues that the value of the image was heightened when miracles involving the statue began to occur. One of these wonders involved an oil lamp. In those days the houses were illuminated with oil or the sap of trees that were burned in little lamps. The opened hand of the statue, which was extended with the palm turned upward, was used one night to hold a lamp. Much to the surprise of everyone in the house, the lamp burned continuously without being refilled. This miracle was immediately made known to everyone in the village.

The people also discovered that when the statue was placed in the center of their fields where the rice and corn were growing or where the fish were being dried, birds and animals did not forage as was their custom.

Legend also tells that during threatening typhoons, thunderstorms, floods, plagues or other types of disasters, the people of Cebu had merely to kneel and pray before the statue for the calamity to be averted. When rain was needed for the crops, the people took the Infant in procession to the beach. After dipping the feet of the statue in the water, an abundant rainfall would bless the island.

The miracles attributed to the statue were so numerous, the people called the statue their Bathala, meaning Supreme Being.

After Magellan's failed voyage, four Spanish expeditions arrived between 1521 and 1542, but all met with the same disastrous results. Then Philip II of Spain, for whom the islands were eventually named, appointed an Augustinian friar, Fr. Andres de Urdaneta, a noted cosmographer, to lead another expedition. Appointed military governor of the islands was Don Miguel Lopez Legaspi. The Legaspi-Urdaneta expedition, sailing under the patronage of the Holy Name of Jesus, landed at Cebu on April 27, 1565. Under a flag of truce, Fr. Urdaneta went ashore to negotiate for amicable relations, but the parley failed. In the ensuing battle, the Cebuans fled to the hills, leaving the city in flames.

When the fire died down the next day, one of Legaspi's soldiers, Juan Camus, explored the area and came upon a large native hut spared by the flames. Inside he found a box that contained a carefully wrapped wooden image of the Child Jesus. The left hand held a sphere; two fingers of the right hand were held in blessing. The discovery of the image in one of the few remaining huts of the village was regarded as a miracle and produced a great excitement. Legaspi entrusted the image to the care of the Augustinian missionaries, who placed it on an altar erected in the same house where it was discovered.

The first church of nipa and bamboo was erected by the Augustinians in 1571. The transfer of the statue from the hut of its discovery to this church marks the first Christian procession held in the Philippines. Unfortunately, the church burned to the ground. This was followed by two other structures made of similar materials. Finally, the erection of the present church of hewn stone was begun in 1730. The Santo Nino of Cebu was enthroned there on January 16, 1740 among great festivities that continue to be observed every year.

According to Fr. Casimero Diaz in his *History of the Philippines*, the wonders attributed to the Holy Infant of Cebu are too numerous to mention. Among these miracles was that which took place during World War II when heavy damage was inflicted by American bombers. Although the church where the statue was enshrined was not directly hit, the nearby explosions caused the image to topple over. Instead of shattering on the floor, the holy image somehow became entangled in the embellishments around its votive stand and was miraculously spared injury, except for a small scratch on the face. An Augustinian priest rescued the image and carried it proudly past burning houses to the relative safety of the Redemptorist church in Cebu City. It remained there until the final liberation of the city by American troops on March 27, 1945.

In his unedited *Relation*, Fr. Urdaneta wrote that the image is similar to those made in Flanders. He shares the opinion of many historians that the image was indeed brought to the islands and left there by Magellan. The archives of the Augustinian Monastery of the Holy Infant of Cebu City likewise concurs with this opinion of the statue's origin based on historic documents.

The wooden image is still regarded as a product of sixteenth-century Flemish sculpture. Standing on its bronze platform, which is embellished with pearls and bronze flowers, the statue stands a foot high. Wearing golden boots and with its hands gloved in gold, the Infant raises His right hand in blessing. Dangling from the same hand is a scepter of gold. The left hand holds an orb which is topped with a golden cross that signifies the Infant's worldwide kingship. Golden chains falling from the orb support three large diamonds that were donated by the Infant's devotees. A golden crown was given in 1965 to the Santo Nino by the former first lady of the Philippines, Mrs. Leonila Garcia, during the fourth centenary celebration of the Infant's discovery by the soldier of the Legaspi-Urdaneta expedition. Another golden crown, studded with jewels, is said to have been the gift of Crown Prince Juan Carlos, who is now the reigning king of Spain.

The wardrobe of the Infant is extensive and is kept in the church's museum. Many of the jeweled vestments and capes hang in glass cases. Others are displayed behind glass in frames that encircle the walls. Other cases hold the many costly ornaments that were given to the Santo Nino by many of His devotees.

On festive occasions the Infant wears a belt on which large Spanish gold coins are arranged. Among other ornaments the Infant also wears the famous Toissone de Oro, the Golden Fleece, which was given to the Infant by King Charles III in recognition of its miraculous reputation. This Toissone is a necklace of gold that has square-cut emeralds, garnets, rubies and diamonds.

The clothing of the Santo Nino is changed twice a year by members of the Confraternity of the Holy Child Jesus of Cebu. Known as Camareras, they perform their privileged function by first clothing the figure in from 18 to 20 white garments (resembling the priest's alb) which are made of sheer, costly fabrics or precious laces. These are donated, and when removed, they are distributed to various provinces as relics. A selection among the Infant's many vests is then made and placed on the figure, concealing the many white garments. One of its jewel-decorated capes is then placed on its shoulders. This clothing of the figure is made on the eve of the feast-day fiesta, before the Holy Infant is brought in procession around the city. One week after the fiesta, the robes are taken off in a ritual called the Hubo (meaning "to take off"). Another set of vestments is then placed on the Infant which remains until the time of the next feast-day.

This yearly celebration has been marked by special observances from the time of its discovery in the hut until the present day. A few days before the feast, faithful devotees from all over the

Philippines converge on Cebu to fulfill promises they made to observe an annual pilgrimage to the Infant. Many of the faithful bring their little replicas of the Santo Nino, which are arranged around the altar. After the solemn Mass on the day of the feast, the basilica is turned over to those who perform a dance known as the Sinulog. This dance is performed before the miraculous image, but those in the square in front of the church also participate. This is a pre-Spanish ritual performance which was preserved as a dance during which both petitions and thanksgivings are presented to the Santo Nino. After a sufficient amount of time is given to the dancers, the statue of the Santo Nino, in a glass enclosure, is carried in procession throughout the city, accompanied by dancers in colorful costumes. Also participating is the Archbishop of Cebu, who is joined by various organizations, many of the clergy and thousands of celebrants.

It is due to the Augustinian Order that the Infant of Cebu is so well known and loved. It was the Augustinians who organized the perpetual Novena to the Santo Nino of Cebu which is held every Friday of the year. It is also the Augustinians who supervise all the festivities and the procession of the Holy Image, and it is in the Augustinian church that the Holy Infant is enshrined in a side chapel.

Devotion to the Santo Nino has spread throughout the islands, with many churches and homes enshrining replicas of the miraculous image. The miracles of the Infant take many forms. Epidemics have been checked, protection has been given in battle, ships have been delivered from storms, and cities have been saved from fire. Also, Cebu was once rendered invisible to invaders.

It is said that no problem remains unsolved, no sickness uncured, no pain unrelieved when the devout pray before the holy image or one of its replicas. In the United States, devotion to the Holy Infant of Cebu is propagated by the Rosarian Dominican Sisters of 19292 El Tora Road, Silverado, California, Zip Code 92676, who have replicas of the Holy Infant of Cebu available for purchase.

THE SANTO NINO (Holy Infant) of Cebu, The Philippines, was enthroned on January 16, 1740 in the hewn-stone church pictured above. Great festivities continue to be held each year on that date.

MANY WONDERS are attributed to the Holy Infant of Cebu. When disasters threatened Cebu in the Philippines, the people had merely to kneel and pray before the statue for the calamity to be averted.

WHEN RAIN was needed, the people of Cebu took the Infant in procession to the beach in hopes that by dipping the statue's feet in the water, rainfall would result. The statue is pictured here wearing one of many elaborate costumes.

THE CHILD JESUS OF DÉOLS

Déols, Indre, France
1187

The distinguished Benedictine Abbey at Déols (a suburb of Chateauroux) was founded in the year 917 by Ebbes the Noble. Sometimes called the Breast of St. Peter because of its influence and service to the Church, the Abbey's privileges have been confirmed by 30 Popes. It was in front of this venerable abbey that the spectacular miracle of Déols took place.

A column situated in a place of honor supported a statue of the Blessed Virgin holding the Child Jesus. Here the villagers were accustomed to pause for a moment of prayer. Located in front of the column and the abbey was an area where the people frequently gathered in friendly exchange. Also gathering there during the English occupation were rough English soldiers who delighted in mocking the poor, and especially the people who prayed before the blessed statue.

The miraculous event took place on May 31, 1187 when the English soldiers were engaged in a game of dice. The soldier who lost the game became enraged. To vent his anger, he picked up a large stone and flung it at the statue, breaking off the hand of the Holy Child.

According to the historian Philippe Auguste, a contemporary of the event,

> A stream of blood poured from the arm of the broken image and made a pool on the earth below. The fellow who flung the stone was seized with madness, and dropped down dead on the spot. John Lackland, and Adhemar, Viscount of Limoges, carefully collected the blood and deposited it in a rich chapel erected in England and dedicated to the Virgin.

According to the historian, Rigord, countless cures were effected by the application of this blood.

News of the miracle spread everywhere. The English soldiers who were in Déols, but who were not present at the time of the miracle, took particular interest in the report since one of their own had instigated the phenomenon and died as a result. To satisfy their curiosity that the event had taken place as reported, a company of soldiers went to the spot the next day. Among them was the brother of the English king, who recovered the hand of the Infant Jesus. After picking it up, he wrapped it in his cloak, when suddenly bright red blood began to flow from the stone hand—to the terror of all the spectators.

In addition to these two blood-sheddings, other prodigies are said to have taken place. These were so spectacular that they caused Philippi Auguste, King of France and Richard the Lion Hearted, King of England, to become reconciled for a time.

After the miracle, the statue was removed to a chapel within the abbey church. Dedicated to Our Lady of Miracles, the chapel became the site of numerous pilgrimages in which, through the years, several Popes, a number of future saints and many noblemen took part.

During the French Revolution the abbey was pillaged and plundered. The statue of Our Lady and the Child Jesus was viciously broken and seriously damaged. The disfigured statue was providentially retrieved by an elderly woman, who secretly kept it until peace was restored. After the miraculous statue was returned to the possession of the Church, it was repaired and clothed in elegant garments.

A confraternity which was established in 1187 in memory of the blood-shedding flourished until the Revolution, but was reorganized in 1830. Members of this confraternity, in addition to many pilgrims, commemorate the miracle of Notre-Dame de Déols every year on May 31, the anniversary of the miracle.

During an elaborate ceremony in the year 1899, the Archbishop of Bourges demonstrated the Church's affection for the statue by bestowing precious crowns on the heads of both Mother and Child.

The abbey which figured in the miracle is still in ruins. The statue of Mother and Child is now found in one of the chapels of St. Etienne's Church, where the Child Jesus remains without His hand in sad remembrance of the disrespectful action that took place over 800 years ago.

A SPECTACULAR MIRACLE occurred in 1187 in Déols, France after a soldier flung a stone at the statue above, breaking off the hand of the Child Jesus. Blood flowed from the stone arm of the statue, and the man who had thrown the stone went mad and died on the spot. The next day, when other soldiers picked up the severed hand, it too bled profusely.

7

THE CHRIST CHILD OF ARA COELI

Rome, Italy
1480

Standing approximately three feet tall, this crowned and bejeweled figure of the Child Jesus is venerated in a special chapel of the Basilica of Santa Maria in Ara Coeli which is located on the famous Capitoline Hill in the city of Rome. Legend tells us that here Emperor Augustus saw a vision of the Blessed Virgin standing on an altar of Heaven. During this apparition he received the prophecy that during his reign, the Son of God would be born of a Virgin. As a consequence, the Emperor had an altar built with the inscription: "This is the altar of the Son of God." A fragment of this altar is still kept.

A pious friar carved the statue of the Infant Jesus in Jerusalem during the year 1480 from the wood of an olive tree grown at Gethsemane. According to tradition, when the Franciscan friar discovered that he had an insufficient amount of paint to complete the statue, the rest of the coloring was applied by angels. The artist presented the statue to the Ara Coeli (Altar of Heaven) Church, which his Order had administered for many years.

The statue of the Holy Infant is always clothed in fine dresses and capes which are adorned with jewels. These garments were donated by people from around the world in gratitude for favors received and in testimony of their affection.

Following an ancient custom, the statue is often relieved of its ornaments and carried on request to the bedside of the sick.

The Infant Jesus was solemnly crowned in 1897 at the request of Pope Leo XIII and the Vatican Chapter.

EDITOR'S NOTE: In February of 1994, the Christ Child of Ara Coeli was stolen from the Church of St. Mary's in Ara Coeli in the heart of Rome. Sadly, it had not been found when this book went to press, despite investigation by a special art theft squad.

While the churches in Rome vie with one another in assembling the most beautiful Christmas crib, one of the more beautiful, and certainly the most famous, is unquestionably the one in which this image is located. The statue is placed in its historic crib scene on Christmas Eve. Sometimes the statue is placed on the lap of a statue of the Blessed Mother, but it is more often situated in a manger during the Christmas season.

From Christmas until the Epiphany the church resounds with the voices of the children of Rome who visit the crib to recite poems, sing hymns and play music in honor of the Christ Child's birth.

The statue is apparently revered throughout the world, as evidenced by the many letters requesting graces and relief of temporal cares. These letters are kept at the side of the glass case in which the statue is protected.

Above: THE FAMOUS STATUE of the Christ Child of Ara Coeli (Altar of Heaven), which was carved in 1480 in Jerusalem from an olive tree that grew in Gethsemane.

Page 43: ST. MARY'S CHURCH, where the Christ Child of Ara Coeli was formerly kept.

LADEN WITH JEWELS and wearing a beautiful crown, the statue is pictured here prior to its theft in February of 1994.

AN OUTSIDE VIEW of St. Mary's Church in Ara Coeli, Rome.

8

THE MIRACULOUS CHILD JESUS
OF LORETO

Salzburg, Austria
c. 1630

An ancient miraculous statue of the Child Jesus which originally came from Switzerland is devoutly kept at the Loreto convent of the Capuchin nuns in Salzburg, Austria. The principal personality in its history is Fr. John Chrysostom Schenk, a Capuchin priest who was given the statue by a superior. Fr. Chrysostom was so devoted to his ivory statue of the Child Jesus that he was eventually nicknamed "Christkindl Pater."

The good priest made a wooden carrying case for the statue which enabled him to carry it more easily on his errands of mercy. At times he loaned it to the sick, but if they delayed in returning it, the statue was frequently returned to the good priest in a miraculous manner.

Fr. Chrysostom died a most holy death on November 25, 1634. Because he had so often carried his beloved statue with him on his apostolic errands, the image was well known. It soon became a center of devotion in Salzburg, where it is still venerated under the name Miraculous Child Jesus of Loreto.

—PART II—

MIRACULOUS CRUCIFIXES

9

THE CRUCIFIX OF LIMPIAS

Limpias, Santander, Spain
Late Seventeenth Century

When entering the sixteenth-century Church of St. Peter, attention is immediately captured by the beautiful life-size figure of the crucified Saviour located above the main altar. Arranged on either side of the crucifix, and somewhat below it, are larger-than-life-size figures of the Sorrowful Mother and St. John the Apostle. Believed to have been the work of Pedro de Mena, who died in 1693, the crucifix was given to the church by Don Diego de la Piedra Secadura, who had been born at Limpias in 1716.

The crucifix is a meditation on the sufferings of Our Lord and is thought to portray the Crucified in the final moments of His agony. Measuring six feet tall, the corpus is clothed with a loin cloth that is held in place with a rope. The feet are one atop the other and are pierced with a single nail. The index and middle fingers of both pierced hands are extended as though giving a final blessing. The face of Our Lord is of particular beauty, with its eyes of china looking toward Heaven so that, for the most part, only the whites of the eyes are visible.

The first recorded miracle involving this crucifix took place in 1914, five years before the grand miracles of 1919. The recipient of the favor was Don Antonio Lopez, a monk belonging to the Order of the Pauline Fathers who conducted a college in Limpias. His entire account reads as follows:

> One day in the month of August, 1914, I went into the parish church of Limpias, by order of my friend D. Gregorio Bringas, to fix the electric light over the high altar. In order to be able to work more comfortably I put two large cases on the altar, and on them a ladder, the ends of which I leaned against the wall that serves as a background to the figure of the Crucified One.

After I had worked for two hours, in order to rest myself a little I began to clean the figure so that it could be seen more clearly. My head was on a level with the Head of the Christ, and at a distance of only a couple of feet from it. It was a lovely day and through the window in the sanctuary a flood of light streamed into the church and lit up the whole altar. As I was gazing at the crucifix with the closest attention, I noticed with astonishment that Our Lord's eyes were gradually closing, and for five minutes I saw them quite closed.

Overwhelmed with fright at such an unexpected spectacle, I could still hardly quite believe what I saw, and was about to come down from the ladder. Notwithstanding, my bewilderment was so great that my strength suddenly failed me; I lost my balance, fainted, and fell from the ladder onto the edge of the altar itself and down the steps into the sanctuary.

After I had somewhat recovered, I was convinced from where I lay that the eyes of the figure on the crucifix were still closed. I pulled myself together hastily and went out in order to relate what had happened, and also to be medically examined, for my whole body was in great pain from the fall.

A few minutes after I had left the church I met the sacristan, who was just going to ring the Angelus, as it was twelve o'clock noon. When he saw me so agitated and covered with dust he asked if anything had happened to me. I told him what had occurred, whereupon he said he was not surprised as he had already heard that the Santo Cristo had closed His eyes on one other occasion, and that it was probably brought about by the working of some interior mechanism.

I asked him to collect the tools together and to put away the ladder, and generally to tidy up everything again. Then when I reached the college I told the Fathers the whole of the above incident. I was examined, but no wounds were found on my body and no broken bones, only a few bruises of slight importance.

Thinking that the movement I had observed in the eyes of the figure was to be attributed in any case to a mechanism, I attached no further importance to the vision, but tried, however, to find out on what occasion this fact had already been observed, but without success, as no one could give me any information whatsoever about the matter.

Since then I have often cleaned the crucifix, and at the same time examined it minutely, and am convinced that there is neither a spring nor any other mechanism on it. What is more, the eyes were so firmly fixed that even by pressing hard with one's fingers they could not be made to move in the least, nor could they be turned in any direction, as I have proved myself again and again.

At the request of his superiors, Don Antonio Lopez wrote the above account of his experience and kept the matter a secret from outsiders. It was only on March 16, 1920, a year after the many miracles of 1919, that the above declaration was made public.

The little town that is favored with the possession of the miraculous crucifix is located on the River Ason in the northernmost part of central Spain, near the Bay of Biscay. Because of this location, the place was primarily engaged in the fishing industry. During the nineteenth century the fishermen gradually moved their families to homes closer to the waterways and began attending services at two churches that were more conveniently located. Because of this movement of the population, plus a gradual laxity of faith of those who remained near the venerable old Church of St. Peter, the church was practically deserted at the time of the first miracle in 1914 and those that took place in 1919.

To re-ignite devotion to the beautiful crucifix and to encourage attendance at the venerable old church, the pastor, Rev. Thomas Echevarria, decided to accomplish this by means of a mission. After applying to the Capuchin monastery at Montehano, near Santander, two priests were placed at his disposal: Friar Anselmo de Jalon and Friar Agatangelo de San Miguel, both of whom were known for their apostolic zeal and success as missionaries.

Before the start of the mission on March 22, Fr. Jalon noticed that the great chandelier in the middle aisle was hanging too low and asked that it be raised so that visibility would be improved. When workmen were preparing the preliminary work on the roof, they noticed that the beam on which the chandelier was attached was nearly broken in the center so that the chandelier was in grave danger of falling. News of this situation was everywhere reported. Devout gratitude was given to Almighty God that a serious accident had been averted.

There was yet another preservation from harm when, on the fifth day of the mission, the clapper of one of the church bells fell on the square below, missing by some five or six inches a boy who had been playing there at the time.

Both events, which were regarded as somewhat miraculous, not only increased attendance, but also heightened the impression made by the mission sermons so that almost everyone received the Sacraments, including some men who had neglected the Sacraments for years. The two missionaries acknowledged that they had never before held such a successful mission.

On the last day of the mission, Sunday, March 30, while the Archpriest D. Eduardo Miqueli was celebrating Holy Mass, both missionaries were occupied in the confessional. Fr. Agatangelo, however, delivered the day's sermon based on the words, "My son, give me thy heart." (*Prov.* 23:26). While he was speaking, a girl of about 12 entered the confessional of Fr. Jalon and told him that the eyes of Christ on the cross were closed. Thinking that this was the product of the child's imagination, the priest ignored her claim until other children also came to him with the same message. After Fr. Agatangelo finished the address and was about to return to his confessional, Fr. Jalon approached him and told him of the children's claim. Both priests then looked at the crucifix but saw nothing unusual. Presently a man in the congregation shouted for everyone to look upon the crucifix. In a few moments the people confirmed with great excitement what the children had seen. Some of the people began crying, others shouted that they had seen a miracle, others fell to their knees in prayer while others called out to God for mercy.

After the parish priest was called from the sacristy and was told that the eyes of the Crucified were opening and closing and that the figure was turning His gaze from side to side, he, too, fell on his knees to pray. But his prayer was soon interrupted by many of the people who declared that the figure was perspiring and that Fr. Jalon should climb up to the crucifix to verify it. When a ladder was produced, Fr. Jalon climbed up and saw that the perspiration covered the figure's neck and chest. After touching the neck, he looked upon his fingers that were wet with the fluid. As verification of what had taken place, he showed his moistened fingers to the congregation. Once again agitation and excitement gripped the people so that it was a long time before they were quieted.

None of the priests saw the movements of the eyes, but Fr. Agatangelo later saw the miracle several times when he prayed alone in the church at night.

A report of all that had taken place was given by the Archpriest D. Eduardo to the bishop of Santander on April 2, 1919. This report was later published in the *Boletin Eclesiastico* of the diocese of Santander.

The second apparition took place on Palm Sunday, April 13, 1919, when two prominent men of Limpias approached the altar. Speaking of hallucination and mass hysteria as they looked upon the crucifix, one of them suddenly pointed upward and fell to his knees. At once the other man also fell to his knees, crying for mercy and proclaiming his belief in the miracle.

The third apparition took place on Easter Sunday, April 20, in the presence of a group of nuns known as the Daughters of the Cross who conducted a girls' school in Limpias. They saw both the eyes and lips of the Santo Cristo move. At this time some of their students also saw the miracle, as did a group of people who were reciting the Holy Rosary. Their experience was quickly reported to the parish priest.

The manifestations were repeated almost daily from April 24. As can be expected, the church was often filled with people from Limpias and the neighboring towns who were hoping to witness the marvel. Rev. Baron Von Kleist reports that:

> Many said that the Saviour looked at them; at some in a kindly manner, and at others gravely, and at yet others with a penetrating and stern glance. Many of them saw tears in His eyes; others noticed that drops of blood ran down from the temples pierced by the crown of thorns; some saw froth on His lips and sweat on His body; others again saw how He turned His eyes from side to side, and let His gaze pass over the whole assembly of people; or how, at the Benediction, He made a movement of the eyes as if giving the blessing; how at the same time He moved the thorn-crowned head from

one side to the other. Others had the impression that a deep, submissive sigh was wrested from His breast, some believed they saw Him whisper—in short, the most varied manifestations were observed on this crucifix.

One of the first to declare his experience to the secular press was the well-known and highly respected D. Adolfo Arenaza. His testimony was published May 5, 1919 in the newspaper *La Gazeta del Norte,* which was published in Bilbao. He reported that he joined a procession going to Limpias in order to visit the crucifix. While looking through his field-glasses he saw the movement of the eyes four times. He further stated that it could not have been an effect of the light nor an hallucination, since people saw the miracle from all parts of the church. He then asked, "Does Our Lord really move His eyes...I am rather of the opinion that He really does move them, for I have seen it myself."

A group of people from Limpias also came forward with a declaration in which they revealed that each of them

> ...had observed the movement of the eyes of the Santo Cristo in the parish church of Limpias on different days and from different positions. Many of us have seen it more than once, and for us there exists no doubt as to the reality of these movements. Some of us who undersign this letter have even made an affidavit, after having tried to deny the extraordinary facts in the beginning...We are convinced that the Christ of Limpias moves His eyes, because we have seen the movement.

Pilgrimages from near and distant towns began to arrive in Limpias. Newspaper reports detailing accounts of the wonderful crucifix spread the news to all parts of Spain and finally to other countries including the United States. One group, under the leadership of the Bishop of Toledo, Joseph Schrembs, arrived in Limpias from America. By the middle of November, 1919, 66 pilgrim trains had arrived at Limpias. Finally, by the year 1921, the number of pilgrims had increased to such an extent that foreign traffic in Limpias was determined to be greater than the visitors to Lourdes. Crowned heads visited Limpias, as did dignitaries of the Church in Spain including bishops and cardinals. Archbishops also arrived from Mexico, Peru, Manila, Cuba, and other foreign nations. Several albums are found in the sacristy of the church of Limpias. These contain well over 8,000 testimonies of people who had seen the wonderful apparitions. Of these, 2,500 were sworn on oath. Among these witnesses were members of religious orders, priests, doctors, lawyers, professors, governors of universities, officers, merchants, workmen, countryfolk, unbelievers and even atheists.

The first bishop to be favored with an apparition was Don Manuel Ruiz y Rodriguez of Cuba, who went to Limpias following a visit to Rome. After returning home he composed a detailed pastoral letter to the members of his diocese in which he told of the miraculous crucifix. He disclosed that he had seen the figure close and open the mouth, how it moved the head from one side to the other, how the face took on an expression of death. Later he again saw the mouth move. "He shut it very slowly but opened it quickly. . .the closing of the mouth was slow until one lip touched the other."

Fr. Celestino Maria de Pozuelo, a Capuchin monk, visited Limpias on July 29, 1919 and wrote a detailed report that included this statement: ". . .The face presented a vivid expression of pain: the body was a bluish colour, as if it had received cruel blows, and was bathed in perspiration. . ."

In his statement, Rev. Valentin Incio of Gijon tells that he visited Limpias on August 4, 1919 and joined a group of pilgrims who were witnessing the miracle. There were 30 to 40 people, two other priests, 10 sailors and a woman who kept cryng. Rev. Incio wrote:

> At first Our Lord seemed to be alive; His head then preserved its customary position and His countenance the natural expression, but His eyes were full of life and looked about in different directions. . .Then His gaze was directed towards the centre, where the sailors stood, whom He contemplated for a long time; then He looked to the left towards the sacristy with a remarkably stern glance which He retained for some time. Now came the most touching moment of all. Jesus looked at all of us, but so gently and kindly, so expressively, so lovingly and divinely, that we fell on our knees and wept and adored Christ. . .Then Our Lord continued to move His eyelids and eyes, which shone as if they were full

of tears; then He moved His lips gently as if He were saying something or praying. At the same time the above mentioned lady who was beside me, saw the Master trying to move His arms and striving to get them loose from the Cross.

Affixing their names to this statement were the three priests, nine of the sailors and the lady.

The Coadjutor of St. Nicholas Church in Valencia, D. Paulino Girbes, relates in his statement of September 15, 1919 that he was in the company of two bishops and 18 priests when they knelt before the crucifix.

> . . .We all saw the face of the Santo Cristo become sadder, paler, and more bluish-looking. The mouth also was wider open than usual. The eyes gave a gentle glance now at the bishops and then in the direction of the sacristy. The features at the same time took on the expression of a man who is in his death-struggle. That lasted a long time. I could not restrain my tears and began to weep; the others were similarly affected. . .

When the Capuchin monk Fr. Antonio Maria de Torrelavega visited the crucifix on September 11, 1919, he saw blood streaming from the left corner of Our Lord's mouth. The next day, he

> . . .observed anew, only still more frequently, the movement of the eyes, and saw, too, once more that blood was flowing down from the corner of the mouth. . .Several times He also looked at me. Now I felt as if my whole being were shaken violently. . .I stood up, therefore, and changed places three or four times, always observing, however, the same manifestations. . .At about two o'clock, as I was kneeling in one of the central benches, I saw the Santo Cristo gazing at me again, and this so affected me that I had to hold on tight to the bench, as my strength was beginning to fail me. . .I noticed that the countenance changed colour and became bluish and sad. Many other persons who were kneeling round me also observed this. . .Now I verify it; there

is no doubt the Santo Cristo moves His eyes. During my visit I saw the movement of the eyes about fifty times...

The Rev. Tomas Nervi of the Salesian order wrote in his statement that he saw the movement of the eyes, mouth, and chin. At the end of his lengthy testimonial he wrote: "I affirm that all I have written here is true. I am prepared to swear to it, and if it were necessary, would sign it with my blood."

The author, lecturer and Father Confessor of the Church del Pilar in Saragossa, D. Manuel Cubi, submitted his statement of December 24, 1919. In the company of a group of people, he saw the Santo Cristo in a death agony.

> ...One had the impression that Our Lord was trying to loosen Himself from the cross with violent convulsive movements; one thought to hear the death-rattle in His throat. Then He raised His head, turned His eyes, and closed His mouth. Now and then I saw His tongue and teeth... For nearly half an hour He showed us how much we had cost Him, and what He had suffered for us during His abandonment and thirst on the cross.

The Rev. Joseph Einsenlohr submitted his statement on June 18, 1921. After offering Holy Mass at the altar below the crucifix, he sat in the church to attend the Mass being offered by another priest. He wrote:

> After the Santo Cristo moved His head and eyes for a certain time He began to pull at the shoulders, to writhe and to bend, as a man does when he is nailed alive to a cross. Everything was in motion, only the hands and feet remained nailed fast. In the end the whole body relaxed as if exhausted, then took up its natural position again with the head and eyes turned up in the direction of heaven. This whole scene of the dying Saviour lasted from the Sanctus until after the priest's Communion...

Many are the statements submitted by doctors who were, in almost all cases, reluctant to visit the crucifix, but did so at the urging of family or friends.

Dr. D. Maximiliano Orts visited the crucifix with his wife and a group of pilgrims. The church at the time was filled with a throng of people who shoved so rudely that the doctor left the church. Later, while standing about six yards in front of the chancel the following occurred:

> ...In order to satisfy my curiosity, I wished to make an anatomical study of the neck. As I was considering the musculus sterno-cleido-mastoideus, I saw, to my astonishment, a red drop of blood behind the right ear, that wormed its way down, exactly like the little trickle of blood that a leech sucks out when placed for therapeutical reasons in the regio mastoidea; this stream of blood spread itself out until it reached the lock of hair which the artist had put in that place, and there it was dispersed...I rested and reflected and again looked up in the hope that the phenomenon would now have vanished; but it was not so. The blood shone and flowed afresh; I compared it with the blood that welled out of the wound in the left hand (painted blood) and then with that which flowed down from the right side of the breast (also painted blood). The comparison showed me that this blood was black and painted, whereas the other was red and mobile...In order to divert my attention I turned my eyes away from the neck, and directed them to the temples, where I saw grey hair glistening with copious sweat. A few moments later there appears round the hair, in a circle about an inch wide, a dark shadow which covers the whole breadth of the forehead and becomes dark blue; presently this colour gets brighter, then turns red and changes itself in red blood which begins to move, and in the same way as on the neck it is soaked up by the hair, that after this proceeding remains grey and glossy.

To test the manifestation the doctor went into a side chapel, where he studied more closely the anatomy of the statue and the movement of the blood. The doctor continues:

> But the riddle was not solved; the phenomenon on the neck, as well as on the temples was repeated, as

often as I looked up and in an identical manner, so that I was convinced, and involuntarily, though quite naturally, I cried out: "Here there is no possible doubt; it is blood!"

The doctor ended his statement with the following: "I am a Christian, and as such I swear that the foregoing relation adhered strictly to the truth, and that the careful tests to which I subjected my observations have procured me the firm and unalterable conviction of their reality." It was signed July 28, 1919 by Maximilian Orts, Municipal Physician of Pravia since 1878 and Subdelegate of Medicine.

Dr. Fernandez de Alcalde in August, 1919 ended his testimonial in this way: "I am firmly convinced that we are dealing here with things which originate with God, the nature of which remains completely hidden from mankind."

Dr. D. Eduardo Perez y Perez gives us a graphic medical report of what he saw on October 6, 1919:

As I was praying before the crucifix of the Santo Cristo, He looked at me lovingly for nearly a minute...then Christ raised His head, which then remained in quite a peaceful attitude. The muscles of the neck relaxed...the eyes were at the same time wide open and turned upwards...there ensued a violent inhalation with straining of the muscles of the neck, whereby the musculus cleidomastoideus especially stood out, and furthermore the musculi pectorales, the scalenus anterior, and the accessory respiratory muscles, with a considerable dilation of the intercostal spaces, as in the case, for example at the last struggle after mortal wounds...For a moment He appeared on the point of death...then He resumed His customary expression, as the artist had given it to the figure...I must add that during the whole of that afternoon I saw the figure a reddish colour. The following day it was a yellowish or lead colour, as with a dying person...

A report made by Dr. Penamaria was published in the paper *La Montana* dated May, 1920. The doctor described what seemed to be a re-enactment of Christ's death on the Cross. He writes that after witnessing the movement of the statue's eyes and mouth, and after changing locations in the church to verify the miracle, he prayed for a more distinctive proof, something more extraordinary "...that would leave no scope to further doubt, and would give me positive grounds for His miracle, so that I might also proclaim it to all and sundry, and defend it against every opponent, even at the risk of losing my life." He then writes,

> This request seemed pleasing to Our Lord...A moment later His mouth was twisted sharply to the left, His glassy, pain-filled eyes gazed up to heaven with the sad expression of those eyes that look and yet do not see. His lead-colored lips appeared to tremble; the muscles of the neck and breast were contracted and made breathing forced and laboured. His truly Hippocratic features showed the keenest pangs of death. His arms seemed to be trying to get loose from the cross with convulsive backward and forward movements, and showed clearly the piercing agony that the nails caused in His hands at each movement. Then followed the indrawing of a breath, then a second...a third...I do not know how many...always with painful oppression; then a frightful spasm, as with someone who is suffocating and struggling for air, at which the mouth and nose were opened wide. Now follows an outpouring of blood, fluid, frothing, that runs over the under-lip, and which the Saviour sucks up with His bluish, quivering tongue, that He slowly and gently passes two or three times in succession over the lower lip; then an instant of slight repose, another slow breath...now the nose becomes pointed, the lips are drawn together rhythmically, and then extend, the bluish cheek-bones project, the chest expands and contracts violently after which His head sinks limply on His breast, so that the back of the head can be seen distinctly. Then...He expires!...I have tried to describe in outline what I saw during more than two hours...

An extraordinary revelation was observed by Dr. D. Pedro Cuesta in August, 1920. The doctor first tells that he was in the company of a priest, a doctor and a married couple. In the morning, during Holy Mass, his companions saw the miraculous movements but he did not, even though he moved from one position in the church to another. That afternoon he was persuaded to return to the church and saw this astounding revelation.

> When I fixed my gaze for the third or fourth time on the figure I noticed that the fleshy parts entirely disappeared, so that only the skin still remained, a skeleton on which I could have made anatomical studies. The head was completely dried up, until it, like the skin that I had seen, totally vanished. After I had not seen the figure at all for some time it reappeared, but as if mummified, until later on it was also restored by degrees in its fleshy parts. Yes, I observed clearly the formation of a hypertrophy (enlargement) of the head, which then also extended to the remaining parts of the body. Each of these apparitions was repeated twice. At the last stage of the second development I could no longer control myself, but cried out in terror and fled out of the church. A cowardly fear had taken possession of me, whereas I had never before known fear—let my description not be set down to exaggeration. . .I, who was never ill, thought I should die on the spot. The instinct of self-preservation drove me out of the church or I should have had to be carried out as a corpse. So I stumbled out of the church and confessed with my whole heart to the people standing outside: By my reputation as a physician and on my word of honour, I take my oath to what I state herewith, and which I will also certify and ratify with my blood.

So emotionally spent was the doctor that he went on to say: "I felt the necessity of taking some restorative [a tranquilizer]," which he did.

Finally, we will give some of the report made by a medical student, D. Heriberto de la Villa which was published in the paper *Del Pueblo Astur* on July 8, 1919. He first declares "energetically," that ". . .auto-suggestion is quite out of the question, for I did not believe in the miracle when I went." He later went into the church at the urging of a friend and saw the movement of the eyes and mouth. He changed his location in the church to better study the movements and then saw the Santo Cristo

> ...fix on me a terrible look full of anger, which makes me shudder, and I cannot help but bow my head...I look up again and see how He is looking to the right, bowing His head, and turns it to the right, so that I can see the crown of thorns from behind...Once again he turns on me the same angry look which makes such a deep impression upon me that I see myself obliged to leave the church.

Later that day he returned to the church and saw that,

> ...little by little the breast and face became dark blue, the eyes move to the right and left, upwards and down, the mouth opens somewhat, as if He were breathing with difficulty. This I saw for fifteen to twenty minutes...I also noticed that above the left eyebrow a wound formed, out of which a drop of blood flowed over the eyebrows, and remained stationary by the eyelids. After that I saw another drop of blood fall from the crown of thorns and flow over the face. I could distinctly discern it, for it was very red and contrasted with the dark blue colour of the face. Then I saw a quantity of blood drip from the crown of thorns onto the shoulder, but without touching the face. He opened His mouth wide, out of which a white matter like froth welled. At this moment a Dominican priest mounted the pulpit, whereupon Christ gazed steadily at him for five or six minutes...When the preacher ended with the words: "and now, Santo Cristo, give us Thy blessing," Christ opened His eyes and mouth, smiling, and bowed His head, as if He wished to give the benediction in reality. At this moment someone who was standing near me asked me if I would venture to swear on oath to what I saw...Then I recognized that Christ wanted to prove to me the truth of what I saw; He opened His mouth again, out of which froth and blood streamed in

> great quantity and flowed out of the corners of the mouth
> quite distinctly. . .Thereafter I believed that it was now
> my duty to swear upon oath to what I had seen, and
> I did so in the sacristy of the church.

As the medical student mentions, a large book located in the
sacristy was for those who wanted to testify, in an official manner,
to what they had seen. Many others waited until they had returned
home to write a detailed statement, which they then forwarded
to the proper authorities.

It should be mentioned that almost all of those who saw the
miracle felt the need to change locations within the church in order
to verify what they had witnessed. For some, the miracle took
place the first time they entered the church, but might not have
taken place sometime later. For others, the miracle did not take
place the first time, but occurred later in the day. Some did not
see the miracle at all. As one witness testified: "The fact that
these manifestations are seen by some, by others not, cannot be
explained by the laws that are prescribed for nature."

The miraculous appearances of the Santo Cristo were not the
only miracles reported, since there were many miraculous cures.
As of July, 1921 the number of cures reported by celebrated doctors, was estimated at over 1,000. Very few of these cures took
place in Limpias, but rather when the pilgrims returned home
and came in contact with objects that had been touched to the
crucifix.

And what of the church's official position concerning the miracles? Bishop Sanchez de Castro, the Bishop of Santander, in whose
diocese Limpias belongs, introduced a canonical process on July
18, 1920 in which Rome was notified of the miraculous cures and
manifestations. One year and one day later, a plenary indulgence
was granted for a period of seven years to all the faithful who
visited the holy crucifix.

The Papal Nuncio, Msgr. Tedeschini, visited Limpias on September 10, 1921. He prayed before the crucifix and examined it
from all angles. After stating to the clergy and people of Limpias
that the beautiful figure made a deep impression on him, and after
expressing his regret at not being able to stay longer, he congratu-
lated them because, "They were chosen, that the Master should
reveal Himself in such a wonder-working image in their church."

We will conclude with a brief report made by a journalist. After watching the movement of the eyes and mouth he stated,

> I could perceive two movements of the jawbone, as if He were saying two syllables with His lips. I shut my eyes quite tight and asked myself: "What will He have said?" The answer was not long in coming, for in my innermost self I clearly heard the significant and blessed words, "Love Me!"

Perhaps that is why Our Lord performed so many wonders for the eyes of believers and unbelievers. At Limpias He demonstrated the agony of His death and the extent of His love for us, not only to evoke sentiments of pity and repentance, but also to ask, no, to plead with us to love Him in return.

PARISHIONERS AT LIMPIAS (in northern Spain) had dwindled in the early twentieth century. But miracles of 1914 and 1919 associated with the six-foot crucifix hanging in the parish church were to stimulate a resurgence of devotion.

THE PARISH CHURCH at Limpias, interior view.

THE MIRACULOUS CRUCIFIX OF LIMPIAS is a meditation on Our Lord's sufferings and is thought to portray His final moments of agony. Miracles of the Crucifix of Limpias include closing and opening of the eyes, bleeding and movements of the head and facial expression. More than 8,000 people have testified to the phenomena. In addition, over 1,000 miraculous cures already had been reported by 1921.

THE CRUCIFIX OF
OUR LADY OF GUADALUPE

Mexico City, Mexico
1921

After the conquest of Mexico by Hernando Cortez in 1519, Christianity was introduced into the country by the prelates he brought with him from Spain. By the year 1525 missionary work was well underway, principally by the Franciscans, Dominicans, Augustinians and the Jesuits. Conversions were numerous and the Faith flourished. The Church operated in peace until the Mexican wars of independence took place between the years 1810-1821. Little by little, laws began to be passed against the Church through the influence of the Freemasons, an organization that had been introduced into Mexico by Joel R. Poinsset. When the Mexican Constitution was adopted in 1857, separation of church and state was decreed. Under the presidency of church-educated Benito Juarez and his successor, President D. Sebastian Lerdo de Tejada, laws against the Church were stringently enforced, producing a veritable persecution.

Under the various laws, official recognition that was formerly given to ecclesiastical persons and corporations was withdrawn. No religious rite or demonstration of any kind was permitted outside church buildings. The State claimed possession of all church buildings. All religious orders were suppressed, as were all confraternities or organizations annexed to religious communities. According to law, all religious were reduced to the secular state and were forbidden to wear their religious habits in public. Superiors of communities were regarded as state criminals. The laws went on and on. Finally, in 1867, all relations with the Vatican were discontinued.

Despite the restrictions placed on the Church in Mexico, the Faith was maintained. Today, Mexico is regarded as being overwhelmingly Roman Catholic.

Although Mexico's churches were closed around the year 1921, the nation's beloved shrine of Our Lady of Guadalupe remained open for public services. The government apparently hesitated to close the shrine for fear of provoking an insurrection. It has been speculated that enemies of the Church plotted secretly to destroy the Faith by harming the miraculous image of Our Lady. If the image were destroyed, so they thought, the shrine would lose its attraction, and the number of services would gradually diminish until none were held at all.

The plan was put into action on November 14, 1921. His identity remains a mystery, but it is known that an enemy of the Faith carried a large bouquet of flowers to the very altar situated under the miraculous image of Our Lady of Guadalupe. Unknown to church personnel, an explosive device with a timer was hidden in the flowers. The bomb exploded with a great roar. Chunks of marble and masonry flew about, and stained glass windows were shattered; destruction of the altar and the sanctuary was extensive. Thankfully, no one was harmed.

One can imagine that as soon as everyone recovered from the shock, their first concern was for the miraculous image. Much to the relief of everyone, the image remained perfectly intact; in fact, its thin glass covering was not even cracked. Amid cries of amazement, the preservation of the image and the security of the glass were regarded as miraculous.

Yet another miracle became known when it was discovered that the large bronze crucifix which had been positioned directly above the altar and beneath the image was now on the floor. The bomb had exploded with such force that the crucifix had been bent from the impact. The curve of the heavy crucifix attested to the strength of the bomb and reinforced the opinion that the preservation of the image was indeed miraculous.

The man who had intended to destroy the Faith by planting the bomb had failed in his efforts, since the opposite response was produced. A special Chapel of Reparation to the Blessed Sacrament was opened to atone for this outrage and for the many offenses committed against the Church since the adoption of the Constitution in 1857.

Later, to preserve the image from other attempts by the Blessed Virgin's enemies, the miraculous portrait was mounted behind bullet-proof glass.

Persecution of the Church continued. Under the regulations mentioned above and many more that are not noted here, many priests and nuns were martyred, including the saintly Fr. Miguel Pro, who was a victim of a firing squad in 1927. Fr. Pro's cause for canonization was introduced in 1952. He has since been declared Venerable.

We are pleased to note that Mexico's relations with the Vatican were restored in September of 1992, after a span of 125 years. President Carlos Salinas de Gortari oversaw constitutional reforms that ended the most rigorous restrictions on the Church. Clergy can now vote and wear clerical garb in public.

The crucifix that experienced the force of the explosion that was meant for the image of Our Lady is now displayed in the foyer of the new basilica. Resting on a pillow, it is kept in a decorated glass enclosure. Countless pilgrims gaze in wonder at this object that attests to the miraculous nature of the portrait of Our Lady of Guadalupe.

THE TWISTED CRUCIFIX of Our Lady of Guadalupe.

11

THE CRUCIFIX OF GENAZZANO

Genazzano, Latium, Italy
1557

Located only 47 kilometers east of Rome, the city of Genazzano is privileged to have two miraculous images. The one that has garnered the most attention is a fresco portrait of the Blessed Virgin that somehow detached itself from the wall of a church in Scutari, Albania when the city was invaded by the Turks, and was miraculously transported to Genazzano on April 25, 1467. Known as Our Lady of Good Counsel, the image appeared under unusual circumstances before a huge crowd that had assembled for a festival. (The history of this image is given in the companion to this book, *Miraculous Images of Our Lady.*)

The second miraculous image is also a fresco and portrays Jesus on the Cross with the Blessed Mother on one side, and St. John the Evangelist on the other. The city of Genazzano is seen in the background. Described as being a Roman work of the fifteenth century, this portrait of Our Lord is also found in the Sanctuary of Our Lady of Good Counsel and has a remarkable history.

During the papacy of Pope Martin V of Genazzano, the pontiff exempted his native city and the city of Cave from taxes. Later, when Paul III was raised to the papacy, he ignored the earlier exemptions and not only reinstated the taxes, but increased them. When Perugia rebelled against the Pope, Prince Ascanio Colonna and the soldiers of Genazzano joined the revolt. In retaliation, Genazzano was invaded by papal troops under Count Nicolo Orsini on March 25, 1541. During the occupation an extraordinary event took place.

It was the year 1557. The Augustinian papal sacristan, Bishop Angelo Rocca, who was also the founder of the famous Library Angelica in Rome, wrote at the time:

In Genazzano, situated in the territory of Rome, at the time of Paul III the territory was at war. A soldier,

74

playing cards in the public square, lost all his money. He blasphemed God and His Mother and entered raging into the church dedicated to the Blessed Virgin and officiated by the friars of St. Augustine. With his sword he inflicted several wounds upon the forehead, the stomach and the legs of the Crucified who was there above the altar, not without the shedding of blood. The soldier who had profaned and struck the sacred image was at once killed by the other soldiers and his body cut to pieces. But the sword of the blasphemer and profaner was marvelously twisted in such a way that a swordmaker would have had great difficulty to imitate it in a long period of labour. As a souvenir of this impiety and of such a wonder, the sword is kept near the sacred image to the present day.

According to the writings of Padre Angelo de Osigo, we are told that in the year 1640, master craftsman Andrea Barbarano succeeded in straightening the sword by using fire and pounding it numerous times with a heavy hammer. But immediately the sword returned to its twisted form. The sword, still in this condition, is presently kept in a niche to the right of the sacred image.

The Crucified still bears the marks inflicted by the solder. These take the form of slashes and puncture marks.

A SOLDIER in Genazzano, Italy became enraged in 1557 when he lost at a card game in the public square. Charging into the nearby church, he ruthlessly slashed the fresco pictured above. The evildoer was immediately killed by other soldiers. His sword twisted up mysteriously, and in 1640, when a master swordsman painstakingly straightened the sword, it miraculously returned to its twisted condition.

12

THE CRUCIFIX OF
OUR LORD OF THE MIRACLES

Buga, Colombia, South America
1570

Legend reveals that around the year 1570 a poor Indian woman from the small town of Buga yearned to have an image of the crucified Christ for her humble hut. The local priest estimated that the cost would be 70 reales and told her that it would be ordered from Quito, Ecuador, a city known for its sculptors.

The Indian woman worked long and hard as a laundress to collect the money, but then, as she was about to make arrangements for the purchase, she learned that one of her neighbors was being jailed for a debt he could not pay. The debt amounted to exactly 70 reales. With little hesitation, she paid the debt as an act of charity so the man could return to his family.

A few days later, as the pious woman was washing clothes at the Guadalajara River, she saw a wooden object floating on the water. As it floated nearer, she saw that it was a crucifix. Believing that Heaven had provided it as a reward for her charity, she retrieved it from the water and with great happiness took it to her hut. One night she heard strange sounds. Looking about to find the cause, she discovered that the box in which she had placed the crucifix was growing larger. To her amazement she found inside the box, not the crucifix she so easily had drawn from the water and carried home, but one that was much larger.

The mysterious growth of the crucifix attracted the attention of her neighbors, who began to venerate it in the woman's hut. Everyone thought the proper place for the crucifix would be a chapel built at the place of discovery which would be, of all places, the very center of the river. This was, of course, an impossibility, but then another wonder took place when heavy rains swelled the river to such an extent that the river changed its course. The change in direction was regarded as miraculous and as a clear sign that Heaven agreed with the planned location for the chapel.

Papers in the city archives reveal that the image was greatly venerated in 1573, three years after its discovery. Because of the many
miracles performed through the merits of the crucifix, it soon became
known as El Senor de los Milagros, the Lord of the Miracles.

News of the miracles reached the bishop of Popayan, in whose
jurisdiction Buga belonged. An ecclesiastical inspector was sent
in 1665 to verify the authenticity of the healings that had taken
place before the crucifix. Twenty-two witnesses gave testimony under
oath of the prodigious nature of the events they had witnessed.
Among the witnesses was Maria Luisa de la Espada, the daughter
of one of the city's founders.

Maria Luisa testified that around the year 1610, when she was
a child, someone in authority gave orders to burn the image since
it was then in very poor condition. The faithful, it seemed, were
in the habit of taking pieces of wood from the crucifix to keep
as relics. In obedience to the order a fire was set and the image
thrown into it. To everyone's dismay, the image refused to burn.
Instead, it began to sweat profusely. This unusual occurrence continued for two days. Maria Luisa, together with countless people,
collected the moisture with pieces of cotton.

The custodians of the shrine do not hesitate to note the inexact
anatomical proportions of the figure of Our Lord. Yet its sorrowful
attitude and bleeding wounds inspire devotion and pity. The figure
of the Crucified measures exactly 4 feet 3 inches. The cross itself
measures at least 7 to 8 feet in height. Around the year 1748,
the image was covered with a material similar to plaster to protect
it from termites.

The first chapel built for the image was repeatedly enlarged until
an elaborate shrine was begun sometime after the Redemptorist
Order came to the area in 1884. Helped by many devout people,
but especially by the local parishioners, construction was started.
The cornerstone was put into place on August 2, 1892. The church
was completed in 1907 and was consecrated the same year on Aug. 2,
the anniversary of its symbolic beginning. Thirty years later, due
to the popularity of the image, the church received the title of
Minor Basilica.

Representatives of the shrine report that the devout can be found
praying before the holy image at all times, and pilgrimages take
place year round without interruption.

It is said that the hope and aim of every visitor to the shrine is to climb the granite and marble stairs that lead to the camarin, the little chapel located above and behind the main altar. The camarin can accommodate 50 people and is arranged so that the crucifix is seen by the faithful in the church. The crucifix is enshrined behind bullet-proof glass. This protection is necessary to prevent its destruction by enemies of the Faith, who have attempted to harm it on more than one occasion.

A special observance takes place every seven years. Known as Rogativas, or public prayers, the event is celebrated with dancing and fireworks. Solemn services are observed inside the church, with several bishops in attendance from different parts of Colombia. Formerly the crucifix was taken outside the church to plead for an end to a drought, or an infestation of locusts, or to quiet other disasters. Now it is taken out of the church only on the last day of the Rogativas. For this event it is carried on a platform that is decorated with orchids. It is estimated that several thousand people visit the city to take part in the services.

A building situated across the street from the basilica displays ancient religious curiosities, including votive offerings and painted plaques that tell in picture form the favors received by the pilgrims.

One of the items displayed is a knife broken into several pieces. The knife was taken into the church by a man who intended to kill the priest who was celebrating Holy Mass. It was a day in March, 1956, before hundreds of worshipers, when the man dashed into the sanctuary and raised the knife to strike the priest. Before the knife struck, it shattered into pieces, so that the man hit the priest only with the handle.

Information from the shrine points out that in addition to various favors received at the shrine, another kind of miracle is noted: "These being of an invisible kind which take place before the many confessors who continuously listen to hundreds of repentant people."

FOUR HUNDRED YEARS have not diminished devotion to the Crucifix of Our Lord of the Miracles; the devout can be found praying before the holy image at all times. Around the year 1610, the crucifix refused to burn when set afire, but in response, the image of Our Lord sweat profusely for two days.

SEÑOR DE LOS MILAGROS
BUGA

A PIOUS WOMAN found the Crucifix of Our Lord of the Miracles floating in the Guadalajara River just days after she had charitably given away money she had saved to buy an image of the crucified Christ.

THE INTERIOR OF THE BASILICA of Our Lord of the Miracles, located in Buga, Colombia, South America. The people's desire to build the church in the middle of the river was approved by Heaven when the river miraculously changed course, accommodating construction of the church.

— 13 —

THE CRUCIFIX OF
OUR LORD OF THE POISON

Mexico City, Mexico
Seventeenth Century

The almost life-size figure of the crucified Saviour which was enshrined above an altar in the Dominican church named Porta Coeli was customarily visited by a holy priest whose name has been lost to us. After praying before the seventeenth-century image, the priest always finished his devotions by reverently kissing the feet of the Crucified.

One day, while an enemy of Christianity prowled about the church, he saw the priest devoutly kissing the feet of the image of Our Lord. After learning that it was the custom of the holy priest to visit the crucifix each day and kiss it, the scoundrel devised a sacrilegious plan. When the church was empty, the enemy stole inside and approached the crucifix. Taking from his clothing a bottle and a small cloth, he carefully poured a liquid onto the cloth and then rubbed the cloth on the feet of the Crucified. The liquid was a deadly poison whose effects had been proven to be almost instantaneous.

When the cleric next visited his beloved Crucifix he prayed, as was his custom, and then approached the feet for the usual kiss. But, as he prepared to kiss the image, the Crucified, always a flesh color, turned immediately to jet black. Horror-stricken at the sudden change, the priest stood motionless while the witnesses, thoroughly terrified at what they had seen, rushed outside to notify the people in the street.

When word of the miracle reached the ears of the would-be-assassin, he hurried to the church in disbelief. Upon seeing the image he fell to his knees beside the priest, and with tears of repentance told the priest of his actions. He asked forgiveness, received absolution and thereafter led a virtuous and holy life.

As a result of the miracle, the people had an even greater devotion to the image. Not only did it receive the homage of the people in the city, but countless others also came from outlying areas to offer their veneration and love.

The holy Crucifix still receives the devotion of the Mexican people, but it especially attracts the attention of countless pilgrims who visit it after acknowledging their love and devotion to the image of Our Lady of Guadalupe.

The miraculous image of Our Lord of the Poison is found in a beautiful side chapel in the Catedral Metropolitana De Mexico in Mexico City.

A POISONING ATTEMPT was foiled when the Crucifix of Our Lord of the Poison instantly turned black in color.

THE HISTORY of the Crucifix of Our Lord of the Poison is illustrated in the above sketches by an unknown artist. Top left: A faithful priest prays before the crucifix, concluding his devotions by kissing the Crucified Christ's feet (top right). Above left: A scoundrel applies deadly poison to the feet. Middle right: The figure of Our Lord turns black, miraculously warning the priest of the foul play. At right: The evildoer repents.

THE CRUCIFIX OF VOLTO SANTO

Lucca, Tuscany, Italy
Eighth Century

The wooden crucifix known as Volto Santo (Holy Face) was also known in earlier times as the Holy Cross. It is reverently enshrined in a free-standing, small octagonal structure (Tempietto) located in the north aisle of the cathedral dedicated to St. Martino in Lucca, Italy. Surrounding the holy figure are countless silver and gold hearts, crosses, rings, pins and medallions which were offered as tokens of appreciation for the miracles and favors received from the wonder-working image.

An ancient legend tells that the crucifix was carved from a cedar of Lebanon by a man named Nicodemus. The legend also reveals that the Italian Bishop Gualfredo, while he was a pilgrim in the Holy Land, obtained possession of the Volto Santo and embarked with it in a boat without a crew or sails. Finally, after miraculously escaping pirates, the boat drifted through the Mediterranean and went ashore on the beach at Luni, near La Spezia. As the worshippers at Luni and Lucca disputed possession of the holy image, the Bishop of Lucca decided to leave the choice of its final destination to the Divine Will. Placing it on a cart driven by oxen, the animals—of their own accord—set off for Lucca. This is said to have taken place during the eighth century.

The first miracle performed by the Volto Santo involved a poor minstrel who had come from France as a pilgrim. Unable to present the image with an offering, he was despondent, but then decided to offer what he had. As best he could, he began to play his lute in front of the holy image. When the humble performance was completed, the image, as a token of appreciation, let fall one of its silver slippers, dropping it in front of the minstrel. Accepting this gift from the Crucified, the minstrel kept the slipper, but was captured a short time later and charged with sacrilegious theft. Judged guilty, his innocence was only established by divine intervention. Since the time of this miracle one of the slippers of the Volto Santo has been supported by a silver cup resembling a chalice.

In the Middle Ages the legend of the Holy Cross and the reports of its miracles spread quickly throughout France, Flanders, London and all the countries visited by the merchants of Lucca.

The image was so well known in England that even the monarchy knew of it. It is said that King William II of England used to swear *"per sanctum vultum de Luca"* ("by the holy face of Lucca").

The Volto Santo eventually became the symbol of Lucca. Its image can be found engraved on the coins of the town and on the seals of the Corte dei Mercanti (the Merchants' Guilds). It is also mentioned by Dante in his *Inferno*.

Disputing the legend previously mentioned, it is the prevailing opinion that the Volto Santo is the work of a Lombard master of the second half of the eleventh century. Extant documents make mention that the Volto Santo was preceded in St. Martino's by another crucifix of which there are no records, except that it is known to have been very old. This might have been the crucifix of the legend.

The Volto Santo has been regarded as miraculous since its arrival in Lucca, a claim that has always been respected.

The holy crucifix was originally of polychrome wood, but the blackening produced during the centuries by the smoke of candles and incense has given the whole figure a very distinctive gloss.

During the annual September festivities in honor of the Holy Cross, the Volto Santo is adorned with precious ornaments: a velvet tunic lavishly decorated with gold embroidery, a tall golden crown, a gold collar and costly ornaments. On the thirteenth of September at sunset, a candlelight procession, attended by the whole of Lucca, makes its way through the town.

FESTIVELY DRESSED, the Crucifix of Volto Santo's right foot is placed in a chalice. This recalls the touching story of the first miracle ascribed to the crucifix (see pages 87-88).

AFTER EXPOSURE to centuries of smoke from candles and incense, the Crucifix of Volto Santo has acquired a distinctive gloss. Annual festivities in honor of the Holy Cross continue to the present time, including a candle-light procession through the town of Lucca on the thirteenth of each September.

SOME CONTEND that the Crucifix of Volto Santo was carved in the eleventh century. Whether the image dates back to the eighth century or even if it did indeed originate 300 years later, there is no dispute that the holy image has been considered to be miraculous during its entire history. During the Middle Ages, reports of its miracles spread far and wide.

THE CRUCIFIX of Volto Santo is reverently enshrined in an octagonal structure in the north aisle of the cathedral dedicated to St. Martino in Lucca, Italy.

15

THE CRUCIFIX OF
THE HOLY CHRIST OF THE SILVERSMITHS

Plateros, Zacatecas, Mexico
Mid-Sixteenth Century

The church in Plateros, Mexico was built in the mid-sixteenth
century, when silver was being mined in nearby Fresnillo and the
capitol city of Zacatecas. Four miles from Fresnillo was the little
town of Plateros, where jewelers and silversmiths abounded. When
the church was built at the height of silver mining, it seemed
appropriate to consecrate the church to El Santo Cristo de los Plateros
(the Holy Christ of the Silversmiths). This dedication was made
known by a sculptured crucifix on the church's façade, as well
as by a large sixteenth-century crucifix that was placed atop the
altar. Elsewhere on the walls of the church were placed images
representing stages of Our Lord's Passion.

Devotion to the holy Crucifix was profound—the people being
sympathetically moved by the graphic marks of the wounds. The
devotion of the people, as well as the many miracles attributed
to Our Lord, became so well known that the history of the image,
as well as the miracles, were documented and are now kept in
the archives of the Guadalajara Cathedral. Other records are kept
by the diocese of Zacatecas and by the Fresnillo Purification Parish.

Through the centuries the miracles performed by Our Lord because
of devotion to His crucified image have been depicted in little paintings called retablos which were given to the Church by the thank-
ful recipients of His favors. These were displayed on the walls
and became so numerous that in 1882, when the Bishop of Zacatecas,
Don Jose Ma. del Refugio Guerra y Alva, visited the church, he
was amazed at the collection and ordered the construction of an
addition to the church that became known as the Altar's Hall, where
additional retablos are displayed.

The Holy Christ of the Silversmiths enjoyed the full attention
of the people until the year 1829, when it began to share this

93

attention with the statues of Our Lady and the Christ Child that were donated by a wealthy mine owner. Known as the Holy Child of Atocha, its history is given elsewhere in this book.

The crucifix of the Holy Christ is found atop the main altar, where it is situated above the niche which enshrines the Holy Child. Here El Santo Cristo de los Plateros receives the love and homage of the people, as He has for over 400 years.

THE HOLY CHRIST OF THE SILVERSMITHS is located in the church at Plateros, Mexico, as is the Holy Child of Atocha (see Chap. 4). The graphic markings on the crucifix inspire sympathy for the suffering endured by Our Lord during His Passion.

—PART III—

MIRACULOUS CRUCIFIXES
IN THE LIVES OF THE SAINTS

16

THE CRUCIFIX OF
ST. BRIDGET OF SWEDEN

1303-1373

We are indebted to two of the Saint's confessors, Peter of Vadstena and Peter of Alvastra, for the biography of the Saint that was written in the year of her death, 1373. From this biography we learn that Bridget was born in 1303 to a mother known for her deep piety and to Birger Persson, a provincial judge who was one of the wealthiest landholders of the country.

At the age of fourteen (or fifteen), Bridget consented to her parents' wishes and was married to Prince Ulf Gudmarsson, who was then eighteen. The happy marriage was blessed with eight children, among them being St. Catherine of Sweden. Apparently Bridget's saintly and happy married life was noticed by members of the Swedish court, since she was summoned there around the year 1335 to serve as companion to the newly married Queen Blanche of Namur, wife of Magnus Eriksson, King of Sweden. It was hoped that the Saint's spiritual practices and kindly disposition would affect the queen, but Bridget eventually realized that she could do nothing to diminish the queen's extravagances or improve her "flighty nature." After an almost six-year effort, Bridget left the court with the love and respect of the royal couple.

When she was almost forty years of age, Bridget joined her husband in a pilgrimage to the tomb of St. James the Apostle in Santiago de Compostella, Spain. On the return journey her husband was stricken with an illness, from which he died three years later. Before dying, he tenderly placed on his wife's finger a gold ring which he said would serve to remind her of their mutual and undying love.

Now widowed, Bridget divided her husband's estate among her children and devoted herself entirely to prayer, penance and religious undertakings. The visions which the Saint had started to experience during her youth now became more frequent.

During the year 1346, St. Bridget founded a monastery at Vadstena for an order of nuns known as the Brigittines, or the Order of St. Saviour. The monastery was richly endowed by King Magnus and was governed by the Saint's daughter, St. Catherine of Sweden.

To seek confirmation of the order, St. Bridget journeyed to Rome in 1349 in the company of her saintly daughter. With the exception of a few pilgrimages, notably one to the Holy Land, St. Bridget remained in Rome for the next 24 years, until her death in 1373.

During her stay in Rome, the Saint might have frequently recalled a vivid dream or vision she had experienced during her childhood in which she saw Our Lord hanging upon His Cross. The Crucified's voice seemed to say, "Look upon Me, My daughter." The child asked, "Who has treated You in this manner?" The vision replied, "They who despise Me, and are insensible to My love for them." This dream was probably remembered numerous times during her many visits to the basilica of St. Paul's-outside-the-Walls. In this basilica is still found the life-size crucifix, sculpted by Pierre Cavallini, to which she was particularly devoted and which is said to have spoken with her. At the base of this crucifix is a Latin inscription which translates: "Bridget not only receives the Words of God hanging suspended in the air, but takes the Word of God into her heart. Jubilee year of 1350." The year 1350 is not the year in which the inscription was placed beneath the crucifix, but the year in which the Saint received the communication from the crucifix. Many claim that this communication consisted of the 15 St. Bridget prayers that are found in many prayerbooks.

Pope Urban V approved the Saint's order in August 1370 when he confirmed the Rule of her congregation.

Three years later, after a most edifying and holy life, St. Bridget died in Rome on July 23, 1373. Since Bridget had often visited the Poor Clares and had occasionally found it necessary to beg alms on the entrance steps, she was buried in their church, San Lorenzo in Panisperna, which is located on the summit of the Viminal Hill. A year later, her daughter, St. Catherine of Sweden, conveyed the remains to the monastery Bridget had founded at Vadstena, Sweden. Left at the convent of the Poor Clares was an arm of the Saint that the nuns wanted for a relic, together with the Saint's coat and a prayerbook.

A mere 18 years after her death, St. Bridget was canonized on October 7, 1391 by Boniface IX.

Alban Butler once wrote that "Nothing is more famous in the life of St. Bridget than the many revelations with which she was favored by God. . ." By order of the Council of Basle, the learned John Torquemada, afterwards cardinal, examined these revelations and approved them as being profitable for the instruction of the faithful. This approbation was admitted by the council as being competent and sufficient. Pope Benedict XIV referred to the Saint's revelations when he wrote that, "Even though many of these revelations have been approved, we cannot and we ought not to give them the assent of divine faith, but only that of human faith, according to the dictates of prudence whenever these dictates enable us to decide that they are probable and worthy of pious credence."

The Revelations were printed and distributed as early as 1492. They were said to have been extremely popular during the Middle Ages, and they are still regarded as excellent material for spiritual consideration and meditation.

In addition to St. Bridget founding a religious order and receiving the 15 prayers from Our Lord, the Saint's name is also affixed to a rosary known as the Brigittine beads which consist of seven Our Fathers in honor of the Sorrows and Joys of the Blessed Virgin and 63 Hail Marys to commemorate the number of years Our Lady is thought to have lived on earth.

ST. BRIDGET (BIRGITTA) OF SWEDEN made many visits to the Basilica of St. Paul's-outside-the-Walls, Rome, where the crucifix pictured above has been on display for many centuries. The artistry of the crucifix, sculpted by P. Cavallini, inspires devotion in the hearts of faithful devotees, as St. Bridget herself was inspired; the crucifix is said to have spoken to St. Bridget in 1350.

AN OUTSIDE VIEW of the basilica of St. Paul's-outside-the-Walls in Rome, where the Crucifix of St. Bridget is located.

ST. BRIGITTE
Canonisée au Concile

THE HOLY LIFE of St. Bridget of Sweden was marked by special gifts, as well as great sacrifice and considerable accomplishments. As a child the Saint had a vision of Our Lord hanging on the Cross in which He seemed to say to her, "Look upon Me, My daughter."

17

THE CRUCIFIX OF
ST. CAMILLUS DE LELLIS

1550-1614

Vivacious and troublesome as a child, Camillus was already a compulsive gambler by the time of his adolescence. At the age of 19 he joined his father in the military service and fought in two battles. One of these, in 1571, was that at Lepanto, during which the Christians won over the Turks in what is acknowledged to have been a victory of the Holy Rosary.

After he was discharged from the military, Camillus returned to Italy and gambled away his inheritance and his equipment. It is said that he even took to begging on the steps of the Cathedral of Mafredonia. After taking a position as a mason's helper he came into contact with a Capuchin priest through whose counseling he experienced a complete reform and a rekindling of faith. His entrance into religious life was abbreviated by a recurring ulceration of his leg which had once interrupted his military career. He applied for treatment at a hospital in Rome, but was so dissatisfied with the servants' lack of cooperation and constant unfaithfulness to duty that be began the establishment of an order whose members were to bind themselves by a fourth vow—to the charitable care of the sick and dying. This vow is still made by members of the order, in addition to those of poverty, chastity and obedience.

With the encouragement of his confessor, St. Philip Neri, Camillus commenced studying for the priesthood and was ordained in 1584.

During the early days of his nursing order, when he diligently worked to improve the condition of the hospital which he served as director, many opposed his efforts. One day a scoundrel entered the oratory of the congregation, removed the crucifix from the wall, cast it aside and disturbed the contents of the room. The discovery of the, vandalism greatly troubled the Saint, who reverently removed the crucifix from the oratory to another room. During the night, while complaining and praying before this crucifix, he saw the body of Christ move, detach one arm from the affixing nail and reach toward him. At the same time a voice came from the crucifix with great clarity and spoke words both consoling and reassuring: "Take courage, faint-hearted one, continue the work you have begun. I will be with you because it is My work." The crucifix is now enshrined in the principal church of the order, the Church of St. Mary Magdalene in Rome. Unquestionably one of the most beautiful churches in that city, it also contains the enshrined relics of the Saint.

The Order founded by St. Camillus, the Order of the Clerics Regular Ministers of the Sick (Camillians), always wore on the front of their robes a large red cross which was meant to inspire the sick and dying to sentiments of confidence and contrition. This was the first time the symbol of the red cross was used as a sign of organized charity, almost 300 years before the establishment of the International Red Cross.

The red cross still decorates the front of the habits worn by members of the Order, with smaller versions being distributed to those who request them. Made of felt, these smaller versions measure an inch and a half in length and are blessed with special prayers that were inserted in the Roman Ritual. Their popularity dates from 1601 and is due to an apparent miracle. While the Camillians were busy with the sick during the battle of Canizza, a tent burned in which the brothers stored their equipment. Everything was destroyed except a red cross that had been attached to a religious habit. One of the officers asked for the cross and wore it as a breastplate, remaining unharmed for the remainder of the battle. The smaller versions have been propagated by the millions throughout the world procuring benefits of resignation, conversion or recovery for the sick.

THE CRUCIFIX OF ST. CAMILLUS DE LELLIS. The figure on this crucifix, which is venerated in the Church of St. Mary Magdalen in Rome, is the one which in 1582 detached its arm and comforted St. Camillus de Lellis with these words: "Take courage, faint-hearted one. Continue the work you have begun. I will be with you because it is My work." Camillus was very discouraged at the time because of opposition to his health care reforms. Our Lord's words were instrumental in the Saint's pushing ahead and founding the Order of the Clerics Regular Ministers of the Sick (Camillians).

THE CHAPEL OF THE CRUCIFIX of St. Camillus de Lellis, located in the sanctuary of the Church of St. Mary Magdalen in Rome. The chapel was constructed between 1762 and 1764.

OUR LORD reaches out His arm to St. Camillus de Lellis in the above painting, recalling the vision of the Saint in which the Crucified Saviour said to Camillus, "Take courage. . .I will be with you because it is My work."

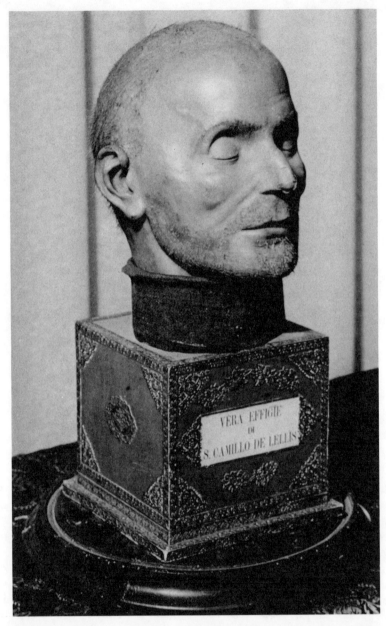

THE VISAGE of St. Camillus de Lellis is captured in this mask, which is located in the church of St. Mary Magdalen in Rome.

THE RED CROSS, seen here on St. Camillus' habit, still decorates the front of habits worn by members of the Servants of the Sick. The artistic rendering of the Saint ministering to the sick brings to mind his determination to assist those who were suffering from illness and destitution, while inspiring them with sentiments of confidence and contrition.

ST. CAMILLUS DE LELLIS is comforted by the Crucified Christ in this painting by Placido Costanzi (1690-1759).

Preceding page: The Infant Jesus of Prague, Arenzano, Italy. See page 11.
Above: The Christ Child of Ara Coeli. See page 41.
Opposite: The Holy Infant of Cebu. See page 30.

112-3

Above: The Crucifix of St. Vincent Ferrer. See page 183.
Opposite: The Crucifix of Volto Santo. See page 87.

Above: The Crucifix of St. Camillus de Lellis. See page 105.
Opposite: The Ecce Homo of St. Teresa of Avila. See page 220.

Above: A painting of the Holy Child of Atocha (Mexico). See page 19.
Opposite: The Crucifix of the Holy Christ of the Silversmiths. See page 93.

Above: Crucifix of Our Lord of the Poison. See page 83.
Opposite: St. Camillus is comforted by the Crucifix. See page 105.

112-10

(Painting by Placido Costanzi)

Above: Another image of the Holy Child of Atocha (Mexico). See page 19.
Opposite: The Holy Child of Atocha dressed as a pilgrim. See page 19.

Above: Our Father Jesus the Nazarene. See page 214.
Opposite: The Crucifix of St. Francis of Assisi. See page 126.
Following page: Crucifix of Our Lord of the Miracles. See page 77.

112-14

THE CRUCIFIX OF
ST. CATHERINE OF SIENA

1347-1380

Catherine was one of 25 children born to Jacomo and Lapa Benincasa, Catherine being the twenty-third. As a child Catherine was very pious and possessed wisdom beyond her years. During her sixth year, while she was on an errand with her brother Stephen, she had a vision of Our Lord near the church of the Friar Preachers in the Valle Piatta. The vision was clothed in pontifical ornaments, a tiara was upon His head, and He was seated upon a throne. Around Him stood St. Peter, St. Paul and St. John the Evangelist. After Stephen roused her from the ecstasy, she cried and said, "O, did you but see what I saw, you would never have disturbed me in such a sweet vision." It was from this time that she seemed to be no longer a child, and her thoughts, her conduct and her virtues were those of one superior to her age. It was shortly after this experience that she decided to join the Order of St. Dominic. Over the vigorous opposition of her mother, she eventually succeeded at the age of seventeen in becoming a tertiary in the Third Order of that illustrious company. She remained in the house of her parents dressed in the habit of the Sisters of Penance and spent three years in seclusion and contemplation. Later, however, she devoted herself to the active apostolate, caring for the sick, visiting and converting prisoners, distributing alms, and attracting to herself disciples who imitated her life of prayer and penance.

During the plague of 1372-1373 Catherine cared for the repulsive sick, prepared numerous people for death, and buried many of the victims with her own hands.

St. Catherine is known to have labored tirelessly for the interests of the Church during its time of schism. She is credited with having persuaded Gregory XI to return the Papacy to Rome from Avignon, where it had been maintained for 70 years. As a result of her exhaustive travels, she brought many rebellious Italian cities back to the obedience of the Holy See. She corresponded with kings and queens for the causes of the Church and prayed and pleaded for Church unity.

Catherine may have experienced all the mystical gifts. She is known to have delivered many from diabolical possession, to have performed many miracles of healing, to have levitated frequently during prayer, to have enjoyed an extraordinary intimacy with Our Lord and His Mother and to have experienced the mystical espousal.

Her prolonged fasts were divinely transformed into a complete abstinence, and while she subsisted only on the Holy Eucharist, her strength and vitality were spiritually maintained.

The Saint was also favored with the stigmata, that is, her body received wounds corresponding to the five wounds Our Lord suffered on the Cross. St. Raymond of Capua, the Saint's confessor and first biographer, was a witness to the extraordinary event when Catherine received the wounds. He writes that the Saint joined him at Pisa where she stayed near the little Church of St. Christina. After celebrating Holy Mass one Sunday and giving Holy Communion to the Saint, the priest noticed that Catherine remained a long time in ecstasy before a crucifix. St. Raymond and others waited for the end of this mystical favor and while watching her they saw:

> . . .her body, that was prostrated on the ground, rise a little, kneel and extend the hands and arms. Her countenance was inflamed; she remained a long time motionless and with her eyes closed. Then, as though she had received a deathly wound, we saw her suddenly fall, and resume a few moments after the use of her senses. She motioned for me and said in a low tone: "Father, I announce to you that, by the mercy of Our Lord Jesus Christ, I bear His sacred stigmata in my body. . .I saw my crucified Saviour who descended upon me with a great light; the effort of my soul to go forth to meet its Creator forced my body to arise. Then from the five openings of the sacred wounds of Our Lord, I saw directed upon me bloody rays which struck my hands, my feet and my heart. . .the bloody beams became brilliant and reached in the form of light these five places on my person."

St. Raymond then asked her if the beam of light reached her right side? She replied: "No, on the left side and directly above the heart. The luminous line that emanated from the right side, did not strike me obliquely but directly...I feel at these five places, and especially in my heart a pain so violent, that without a new miracle, it appears to me impossible to live in this state..."

The crucifix before which the Saint knelt when receiving these wounds is reverently kept.

St. Catherine ranks among the greatest mystics and spiritual writers the Church has produced. She has also been the inspiration and model for many of the Saints who followed her. Venerated as a Saint even during her lifetime, she was solemnly canonized by Pope Pius II in 1461, and in 1939 Pope Pius XII gave to Italy, as its chief patron saints, St. Francis of Assisi and St. Catherine of Siena.

The importance of her writings and spiritual doctrine was officially recognized by the Apostolic See during the solemn ceremonies conducted by Pope Paul VI on October 4, 1970, when she was declared a Doctor of the Church, the second woman to bear this illustrious title.

ST. CATHERINE OF SIENA (1347-1380) was stigmatized before this crucifix.

A favorite subject of painters, reception of the stigmata by St. Catherine
of Siena, is here depicted by the artist Fungai.

AS SHE RECEIVES THE STIGMATA, St. Catherine of Siena kneels before the Crucifix. (Painting by Balducci.)

19

THE CRUCIFIX OF ST. COLETTE

1381-1447

This visionary, reformer, healer of schisms and worker of miracles was born to a poor carpenter of Corbie in 1381 and was named Nicolette in honor of St. Nicholas of Myra, for whom her parents had a special devotion. When both parents died within a short time of each other, Colette was placed under the care of Dom de Roye, the Benedictine abbot of Corbie. Instead of marrying, as he suggested, Colette distributed her belongings to the poor and became a tertiary of St. Francis, taking a vow of seclusion with the permission of her guardian.

On the feast of the Stigmata of St. Francis, September 17, 1402, Colette was immured in a cell between two buttresses of the church named Notre Dame de Corbie. In the wall separating the church and the cell was a small opening through which Colette could receive Holy Communion and attend services.

St. Francis appeared to her and requested that she reform the Order of St. Clare; her confessor encouraged her to leave her cell and seek the authority of the Pope. She turned to Benedict XIII, an antipope, who allowed her to enter the order of Poor Clares and empowered her by several Bulls, dated 1406, 1407 and 1412, to serve as the superior general with full authority to reform the order and to found new convents. The Collettine reform spread quickly from France to Spain, Flanders and Savoy and even influenced the order of the Friars Minor.

In addition to being a reformer, St. Colette helped heal the great schism when there were three claimants to the papacy: Benedict XIII, John XXIII and Gregory VII. Together with St. Vincent Ferrer, St. Colette persuaded the Council to proceed with a new election, after which Martin V was chosen as the legitimate heir to the throne of Peter.

Colette was favored with many visions, especially those regarding the Passion of Our Lord. She was frequently rapt in ecstasy while assisting at Mass and especially after receiving Holy Communion. After experiencing a vision in which men and women in great numbers were falling into Hell, St. Colette became fervently devoted to the Poor Souls in Purgatory and prayed unceasingly for the salvation of souls.

Throughout her lifetime there was one article that St. Colette yearned for, a relic of the True Cross. One day as she was praying, the remembrance of Christ's sufferings drew her into an ecstasy which was witnessed by her companions in religion. When the ecstasy ended she discovered in her hand a small golden crucifix that had not been there before.

The figure of the Crucified is on the front; on the back, immediately behind the head of Christ, is a small golden receptacle containing a red stone. Surrounding this on four sides are four pearls. Four blue stones are situated on the outer extremities, with a fifth pearl added at the foot of the cross.

It was soon discovered that the cross was actually a reliquary. On the front of the crucifix where the figure of Our Lord is displayed, a portion of the cross containing the figure can be turned back, or removed, revealing a relic of the True Cross which is identified with an inscription.

When St. Colette told St. Vincent Ferrer about her experience and the heavenly gift of the crucifix, he held out his hand to receive it. But when he saw it in the hand of St. Colette, he fell to his knees and for a time was oblivious to everything around him.

This precious Cross from Heaven is kept at the Poor Clare convent of Besancon, France.

At the same convent is another precious crucifix, that being the miraculous missionary cross of St. Vincent Ferrer.

St. Clare foretold her own death, which took place in 1447 during her sixty-seventh year.

ST. COLETTE, visionary, reformer, healer of schisms and miracle-worker, is seen here in an engraving by Michel van Lochom circa 1639.

ST. COLETTE'S "CROSS FROM HEAVEN." St. Colette's lifelong yearning for a relic of the True Cross was answered when the small golden crucifix pictured above miraculously appeared in her hand. The cross is a reliquary; a portion of the front of the cross can be removed, revealing a relic of the True Cross.

20

THE CRUCIFIX OF ST. EUSTACE
(d. 118)

and

THE CRUCIFIX OF ST. HUBERT
(d. 727)

Legend tells that Eustace (Eustachio) was a Roman general under Emperor Trajan who believed that profession of Christianity was a crime worthy of death. While still a heathen, Eustace was hunting one day between the towns of Tivoli and Palestrina near Rome, when he saw a stag coming toward him with a crucifix between its antlers. At the same time he heard a voice telling him that he was to suffer for Christ's sake. He was soon baptized, together with his wife, Tatiana, and their two sons. Unfortunately, due to a number of difficulties, the family was scattered, but later became reunited.

Following a military victory, Eustace was asked to sacrifice to pagan idols but refused to do so. Because of this refusal, he and his family were put to death by being roasted in a heated brazen bull.

Although the incident regarding the stag and the crucifix is considered legendary, veneration of the Saint is very old in both the Greek and Latin Churches. He is honored as one of the Fourteen Holy Helpers and is invoked in difficult situations. Eustace is the patron of both hunters and of the city of Madrid. In Rome, the Church of Sant' Eustachio claims possession of his relics.

St. Eustace was martyred in the year 118; his feast day was formerly observed on September 20.

* * *

A similar event is said to have converted St. Hubert (d. 727) from a worldly life to one of such regularity that he was ordained a priest and later became the Bishop of Liege.

According to the legend, Hubert, who was fond of hunting, was engaged in this pursuit one Good Friday when he saw a stag of great beauty in the forest of Ardennes. The beast turned toward him, displaying a crucifix between its antlers. Hubert stopped in astonishment, as a voice was heard saying, "Unless you turn to Me, Hubert, you shall fall into Hell."

Hubert dismounted from his horse, prostrated himself on the ground, venerated the cross which the stag bore and vowed to abandon the world and consecrate himself to God. After Hubert begged for guidance, the same voice told him to seek out Lambert, the Bishop of Maestricht, who would introduce him to a life of virtue.

The authenticity of this vision is questioned by many who believe that the account of the stag of St. Eustace probably evolved into the history of St. Hubert because of Hubert's fondness for hunting and his designation as the patron of hunters.

A DEER'S ANTLERS framed the Crucified Christ in the vision that converted St. Eustace (d. 118). The Saint is one of the Fourteen Holy Helpers and is invoked in difficult situations.

THE VISION OF ST. HUBERT (d. 727) also included a crucifix-bearing animal and resulted in a dramatic conversion. St. Hubert is the patron of hunters.

21

THE CRUCIFIX OF ST. FRANCIS OF ASSISI

c. 1181-1226

The Church's first stigmatist, who was also the founder of the world's largest religious order, was born at Assisi, the son of a wealthy cloth merchant. He was uninterested in his father's business and in formal learning, but took great interest in adventure and romantic chivalry. Eventually turning his back on the world, he wedded, as he said, Lady Poverty. His way of life became clear to him on the feast of St. Matthias in the year 1209 when the gospel of the Mass read, "And going, preach, saying: The kingdom of heaven is at hand...Freely have you received, freely give...Do not possess gold...nor two coats nor shoes nor a staff...Behold I send you as sheep in the midst of wolves..." (*Matt.* 10:7-16). Applying the words literally to himself, he gave away his possessions, put on a ragged gown that he fastened around his waist with a cord, and went about preaching the Gospel.

Known as "the Poverello," St. Francis one day wandered into St. Damian's church, which was then in a sorry state of disrepair. Kneeling before the Byzantine cross with its painted image of the crucified Saviour, the Saint prayed, "Great God, and You, my Saviour, Jesus Christ, dispel the darkness of my soul, give me pure faith, lasting hope and perfect charity. Let Thy Will, O God, be my will; make me and keep me Thine, now and forever."

In response, a voice sounded from the crucifix and repeated three times, "Francis, go and repair My house which you see is falling down." Understanding the words to mean the church building in which he was praying, and not the Universal Church, which many believe was intended, he secured funds for the necessary building materials by selling bolts of fabric from his father's store. This indiscretion placed him on the shadowed side of his father's disposition and instigated his disinheritance.

Out of humility, Francis gave his order the name of Friars Minor. The Order he founded for women with the help of St. Clare became known as the Poor Clares. People in the world who wanted to advance in spirituality under the influence of the Franciscan Order were not forgotten, since the Third Order was established about the year 1222, 10 years after the founding of the Poor Clares.

The custom of making a crib scene at Christmas time was probably not unknown during the lifetime of St. Francis, but his use of it is said to have begun its subsequent popularity.

St. Francis received the stigmata on Mount Alvernia in 1224 and died on October 3, 1226.

The first church of the Order, the small Portiuncula which measures 22 feet by 13-1/2 feet, stands beneath the cupola of the Basilica of Santa Maria degli Angeli in Assisi, Italy.

ST. FRANCIS OF ASSISI

ST. FRANCIS OF ASSISI knelt and prayed before the Byzantine crucifix pictured here; he was answered by a voice which sounded from the cross and repeated three times, "Francis, go and repair My house which you see is falling down." The crucifix is kept at the Basilica of St. Clare in Assisi, Italy.

THE PORTIUNCULA, pictured above, is the first church of the Order founded by St. Francis. The 22- by 13.5-ft. structure stands beneath the cupola of the Basilica of Santa Maria degli Angeli in Assisi.

22

THE CRUCIFIX OF
ST. FRANCIS DE GERONIMO

1642-1716

Born in the small town of Grottaglie, Francis enrolled at the age of sixteen at the college in Taranto which was conducted by the Society of Jesus. Since Francis was so successful in his studies, the bishop sent him to Naples to attend the celebrated college of Gesu Vecchio, which at that time rivaled the greatest universities in Europe. He was ordained there on March 18, 1666. After teaching four years Francis entered the novitiate of the Society of Jesus. Following his first year's probation, Francis was sent with an experienced missionary to Otranto to receive his first lessons in the art of preaching. The next four years were spent preaching and giving retreats and missions. His gift for preaching was promptly noticed by his superiors, who first allowed him to complete his studies and then sent him to Naples to reside at the Gesu Nuovo, the residence of the professed fathers. Naples became his field of apostolic labors for the next 40 years, until his death.

Francis was an indefatigable preacher who proclaimed the gospel in the streets, the public squares, in the low quarters of the city and the churches. His sermons touched guilty consciences and worked miraculous conversions.

The Saint customarily chose those areas where there was scandalous activity. One day he took his position before a notorious brothel in Naples while a great crowd gathered around to hear him preach. While he was proclaiming the word of God, a carriage drawn by two horses tried to pass through the gathering, but was stopped. The gentlemen within the carriage called to the coachman to drive on, but the Saint, holding out a crucifix, cried aloud, "O holy Jesus, if these infidels have no respect for Thee, let their horses teach them better." As he spoke, the horses fell on their knees and continued in that position until the sermon was over.

When Francis preached, he seemed to acquire a power that was more than natural, and his feeble voice became resonant and awe-inspiring. He was often seen walking through the streets of Naples with a look of ecstasy on his face so that his companions had to constantly call his attention to the people who greeted him. He had the reputation of being a miracle worker with the gift of healing.

Upon his death everyone spoke of his holiness, his zeal, eloquence and inexhaustible charity. His heroic virtues were also recognized by Pope Gregory XVI, who canonized the Saint on May 26, 1839.

ST. FRANCIS DE GERONIMO preached with crucifix held high, his feeble voice resonant and awe-inspiring. The Saint had the reputation of being a healer and miracle worker.

23

THE CRUCIFIX OF ST. FRANCIS DE SALES

1567-1622

After receiving an excellent education at Paris and Padua, Francis declined the worldly plans made for him by his father and instead decided on a priestly vocation. The Saint's brilliant preaching, wise direction of souls and his countless conversions brought him to the attention of Church officials, who appointed him Bishop of Geneva in 1602.

Among his friends were St. Vincent de Paul and St. Philip Neri. St. John Bosco, who is described as the wonder-worker of the nineteenth century, admired St. Francis de Sales so much that the order he founded, the Salesians, was named for this saintly bishop. Together with St. Jane Frances de Chantal, Francis founded the Order of the Visitation, of which there are now 185 monasteries throughout the world.

In his biography of the Saint, Hamon, a priest of St. Sulpice, tells that one day when St. Francis returned to Annecy, he retired to the Jesuits' college to prepare a sermon which he was to deliver in the church of St. Dominic. We are told that it was a cloudy day and rather dark in the church when the Saint climbed into the pulpit. Then,

> . . .as he began to preach, the crucifix shed such rays
> of light upon him that his person seemed dazzling and
> his face was brighter than the stars. All the audience
> cried out in surprise and admiration, but the preacher
> stood unmoved. He preached with such power of the
> Holy Ghost that many were converted, and his success
> only increased as he went to the other churches.

Known for his gentleness and patience, the Saint died during his 56th year, the 20th of his episcopate. Attended by numerous miracles, the body of the Saint was buried at Annecy in the first monastery of the Visitation Order, where it is still found beside the reliquary containing the remains of St. Jane Frances de Chantal.

The holy Bishop was canonized in 1665 and was declared a Doctor of the Church in 1877 in view of his excellent writings, of which *Introduction to the Devout Life* and *Treatise on the Love of God* are the most popular.

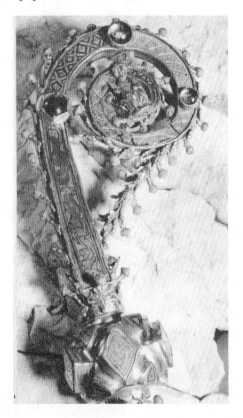

Photo: René Perrin

ST. FRANCIS DE SALES' CROSIER. The bishop's crosier of St. Francis de Sales, which is symbolic of his pastoral office, responsibility and authority.

THE CRUCIFIX of St. Francis de Sales issued dazzling light as the Saint began to preach a sermon on Good Friday, 1606, in the church of St. Dominic of Chambery. The rays of light which shone on the orator were visible to the congregation, causing many to cry out in surprise and admiration.

Photo: René Perrin

ST. FRANCIS DE SALES (d. 1622), a Doctor of the Church, is famous for his devotional writings, which include *Introduction to the Devout Life* and *Treatise on the Love of God,* as well as several other volumes. The Saint, together with St. Jane Frances de Chantal, founded the Visitation Order. St. Francis de Sales is the patron saint of journalists and other writers.

— 24 —

THE CRUCIFIX OF ST. GEMMA GALGANI

1878-1903

Gemma's mother, Aurelia Landi Galgani, was a devout Catholic; her father, Enrico Galgani, an apothecary, was a member of the family of St. John Leonardi. Seven children joined the Galgani family of which Gemma and her brother Gino, who wanted to become a priest, were the most outstanding.

After her mother's death at the age of 39, Gemma became the little mistress of the household, teaching her young siblings and performing the household chores. Her eldest brother, at the process of her beatification, declared that Gemma "was careful in household matters, being fond of needlework and genuinely woman-like in all her ways, except in one respect: her indifference to dress and all personal adornments, which had been great, but which during this period of her life turned into actual severity of rule, supernatural reason accounting for it."

In fact, for the greater part of her life Gemma wore a perfectly plain black dress, with no collar or lace of any kind, and a black cloak and a straw hat for going out. It is said that such severity of dress was the more striking in her, "because she had a beautiful face and a graceful figure."

As the result of extending too much credit, her father lost his business and died soon after in November of 1897. Gemma and her siblings were left destitute, but somehow managed to survive.

Soon after, Gemma was struck with a terrible illness that settled in her back. Some have said it was meningitis, others claim it was tuberculosis of the spine. After suffering a long time from the disease and many complications, and after enduring a number of operations without anesthetic, Gemma was miraculously cured after making a novena to St. Gabriel Possenti and St. Margaret Mary.

Her first vision of Our Lord took place on Holy Thursday, 1899. Many such visitations followed, as did those of the Blessed Mother and Gemma's guardian angel, who was her constant companion

137

and comforter. She conversed with him in a low, sweet voice and he revealed to her the deepest mysteries of the Faith. During that same year, on June 8, 1899, which was then the eve of the Sacred Heart feastday, she received the stigmata, the marks of Our Lord's five wounds. From then on, she began to suffer and bleed from the wounds every week from Thursday night to Friday afternoon. At her confessor's command she asked Our Lord to remove the visible marks of these wounds. He did so, but the sufferings remained. For a time she suffered the most furious assaults of the devil because of prayers she recited for the salvation of hardened sinners.

During the month of September, 1900, Gemma began living with a devout family in Lucca named Giannini. Here she would often come in contact with the priests of the Passionist Order, since the Giannini household had rooms at their disposal. In this house she became a useful member of the family, an elder sister to the young children, and a good hand at household chores.

In the dining room of this house was a long table, simple furnishings, and on the wall a full-size crucifix that was highly venerated by the whole family. During the day Gemma would pause for a visit and sometimes, when Gemma was overwhelmed by a burning wish to kiss the wound on Christ's side, she found herself miraculously raised from the floor. With her arms around the crucifix, she pressed her lips against the sacred wound of Our Lord's side. During the month of September 1901, while preparing the table for a meal, she turned to contemplate the holy crucifix. Suddenly Gemma was raised up. As the figure of Jesus became animated, He detached His right arm from the cross and embraced her, and with a loving gaze He invited Gemma to embrace Him in return. During the entire time of this loving communion, Gemma was elevated, without support, several feet above the floor.

Gemma lived in the Giannini home for almost four years. It seems unbelievable to read in an Italian biography of the Saint that the wonderful gifts Gemma experienced were little known in the family and that those who knew of them almost completely ignored them. Only one person seems to have taken an interest, her confidant, a woman of the household whom Gemma called Aunt Cecilia.

Gemma had always wanted to join a religious community, especially the Order of the Passionists. Unable for various reasons to become a member, she once said that since they would not have her in life, they would have her in death. The prophecy was realized. First buried in the public cemetery, her relics now rest in the chapel of the Passionist Sisters in Lucca. Her tomb bears the following inscription:

> Gemma Galgani from Lucca, most pure virgin, being in her twenty-fifth year, died of consumption but was more consumed by the fire of divine love than by her wasting disease. On the eleventh of April, 1903, the vigil of Easter, her soul took its flight to the bosom of her celestial Spouse. Oh! Beautiful soul! In the company of the angels.

In time, the Giannini house was turned into a sanctuary. The miraculous crucifix still hangs in the dining room, where thousands of pilgrims bend the knee and meditate on the sufferings of the Divine Redeemer and on the sufferings endured by the little mystic.

Gemma Galgani was canonized by Pope Pius XII in May, 1940.

ST. GEMMA GALGANI

ST. GEMMA GALGANI was readying a table for a meal in the Giannini household when the crucifix on the wall seemed to come alive. Gemma was miraculously raised several feet above the floor, and the figure of Christ detached its right arm and embraced her.

STIGMATIST St. Gemma Galgani was furiously assaulted by the devil because of prayers she recited for the salvation of hardened sinners. The holy virgin died of consumption at the age of 25.

25

THE CRUCIFIX OF
BL. JAMES OF BEVAGNA

1220-1301

From the day of his birth in the year 1220, when brilliant stars announced his birth, Bl. James' future holiness was predicted by all who knew him. When he was still very young, the reconciliation of two warring families, the Bianconi and the Alberti, was attributed to his pious prayers.

When James was sixteen, two Dominican friars arrived in Bevagna to conduct Lenten services. Inspired by their sermons, James reflected on the possibility of a religious vocation and opened his heart and soul to one of the friars. Three recommendations were made: that he spend the night before the Blessed Sacrament asking for light, that he fast during Good Friday on bread and water, and that he await the will of God. During the night, after experiencing a dream in which St. Dominic told him, "Do it! According to God's will I choose you and will be ever with you," James left with the friars to join their order at Spoleto.

James was clothed in the habit of the Dominican Order, and was soon professed and eventually ordained. After teaching theology at Orvieto, James was given permission to establish a house of the Order in his hometown. In addition to the labors involved in this undertaking, as well as those of serving the community as prior, he worked with energy at eliminating a recurrence of heresies that were active in the territory. His preaching was inspired, and his gifts at reconciling enemies and bringing peace between families and cities was remarkable.

James' adherence to holy poverty was strictly observed and was well known, especially involving an incident concerning his mother. On one occasion when she saw him clothed in his tattered habit, she gave him money to buy a new one. Since he wanted very much to have a crucifix in his cell, he obtained permission from his superiors to purchase a crucifix instead of the habit. The next time his mother saw him still wearing the worn habit, she reminded him of the money she had given him. James is said to have replied with the text: "Put ye on the Lord Jesus Christ," assuring his mother that the crucifix was a better garment than any he could have purchased.

This crucifix was to clothe him in a way he never suspected.

One day, while praying before the crucifix, James was overwhelmed with his unworthiness, and with great dryness of spirit was concerned about his eternal salvation. Begging God to give him some sign that his soul would be saved, a large quantity of blood fell on him when it suddenly spurted from the hands and side of the figure. Immediately a voice from the crucifix was heard to say, "Behold the sign of your salvation!"

This marvel is mentioned in the prayer of Bl. James' office.

The miraculous blood was collected and was preserved for more than two centuries at the tomb of Bl. James, where countless miracles were experienced. Unfortunately, the vial that contained the miraculous blood was stolen by heretics.

Blessed James died on the day he had predicted, August 22, 1301. While his brethren were reciting prayers for the dead, a voice was heard saying, "Do not pray for him, but ask him to pray for you."

The cultus of Bl. James was approved by Pope Boniface IX in 1400. His feastday is solemnly celebrated on August 23, when his incorrupt body is reverently displayed in the sanctuary of the Beatus in Bevagna, Italy.

26

THE CRUCIFIX OF ST. JOHN OF THE CROSS

1542-1591

Regarded as one of the greatest mystical theologians, St. John of the Cross was the son of a poor weaver. During his childhood the Blessed Virgin miraculously saved him from drowning. He received an excellent education and entered the Carmelite Order in 1563. Because of the laxity that existed in the Order, he was thinking of joining another religious family when St. Teresa of Avila encouraged him to introduce her reform among the friars. For several years he was engaged in this work and in acting as confessor to the nuns of the Discalced Carmelite Order.

One day, during the Saint's last visit with his brother, Francisco, John took him by the hand and led him into the garden. When they were alone the Saint related the following, which was recorded by Francisco.

> I wish to tell you something that happened to me with Our Lord. We had a crucifix in the monastery and one day, when I was standing in front of it, it occurred to me that it would be more suitable to have it in the church. I was anxious to have this crucifix honored, not only by the religious, but also by the people. I carried out my idea. After I had placed it in the church as fittingly as I could, and whilst in prayer before it, Christ said to me, "Brother John, ask Me for what you wish and I will give it to you for the service you have done Me." And I said to Him, "Lord, what I wish You to give me are sufferings to be borne for Your sake and that I may be despised and regarded as worthless."

On yet another occasion, a crucifix figured prominently in the life of the Saint. Once when St. John was engaged in contemplative prayer the crucified Jesus appeared to him in a corporeal vision, covered with wounds and blood. Following the ecstasy John sketched the Redeemer in pen and ink on a piece of paper only five inches long, and presented the drawing to his spiritual daughter, the nun Ana Maria of Jesus, to whom he confided the vision.

Because the head of the crucified in the drawing is inclined, the face is not visible, but the shoulders that bore the scourging are prominently exposed. When held sideward the full impact of the drawing is strengthened, since the body drags away from its support with the arms stretched to the extreme. Although its anatomy is "occasionally at fault," it was always highly respected by artists who have studied it throughout its existence. The piece of paper upon which the image is impressed is now quite yellow and is reverently guarded in a golden reliquary at the Convent of the Incarnation in Avila.

Among his many writings the most famous are: *The Ascent of Mount Carmel, The Dark Night, The Spiritual Canticle* and *The Living Flame of Love.* Because of these writings and others, St. John was proclaimed Doctor of the Church in 1926.

ST. JOHN OF THE CROSS drew this sketch following a vision of the crucified Christ covered with wounds and blood.

GRACED WITH VISIONS, St. John of the Cross (1542-1591), a Doctor of the Church, possessed many mystical gifts.

THE CRUCIFIX OF ST. JOHN GUALBERT

d. 1073

As the son of a nobleman, John Gualbert was educated both in religious and secular matters according to his position in life. But upon reaching adulthood, his attention was given to worldly affairs and the comforts afforded by the privileges of his noble status—until his eyes were opened in a remarkable way to the dangers that threatened his soul.

Tragedy had befallen the family when John's brother, Hugh, was murdered by a man reputed to be his friend. As a man of honor, John went in search of the culprit and was one day returning to Florence with his squire when he entered a narrow pass and suddenly found himself face to face with the murderer. The man, seeing that he could not flee, dismounted, held out his arms in the form of a cross, hung his head in prayer and trembled in fear as he waited for the inevitable thrust of the sword. But John, seeing the crucified Saviour in this display and being moved by grace, sheathed his sword, forgave the man and went on his way.

After dismissing his squire, he journeyed on to the church of the Benedictine monastery of San Miniato, where he knelt before a great crucifix. While imploring for merciful forgiveness of his sins, the image of the crucified Saviour bowed its head. John accepted this sign as Our Lord's forgiveness and His approval of the mercy John had rendered his enemy. This miraculous crucifix is now kept in the church of the Santissima Trinita at Florence.

John Gualbert joined the Order at San Miniato and eventually founded his own order of monks known as the Vallombrosans, named for the location of their first monastery. He is known to have miraculously supplied food, and to have had the gifts of prophecy and healing. He died peacefully after receiving the last Sacraments, being 80 years or more. Pope Celestine III canonized him in 1193.

THE CRUCIFIX OF PADRE PIO

1887-1968

Born in Pietrelcina in southern Italy on May 25, 1887, Francis (later known as Padre Pio) was the son of Grazio and Giuseppa Forgione. He was baptized the day after his birth and showed early signs of holiness. At the tender age of five he expressed a desire to become a priest and to imitate the example of his patron, St. Francis of Assisi.

The home of this future friar was a poor two-room house on a narrow street. The main source of support for the family was a few acres of land they owned outside the little town. Of his early days Padre Pio said, "We had little. But, thank God, we never lacked anything."

After graduating from grammar school in 1897, young Francis was placed under the instruction of a private teacher, a retired priest of the town, Don Domenico Tizzani. For a time he studied under Professor Angelo Caccavo, from whom he received the equivalent of a high school education.

Francis next applied to the Order of the Capuchins of the Province of Foggia. He received the religious habit and the name Fra Pio. Seven years later, on August 10, 1910, at the age of 23, Padre Pio was ordained. During the first years after his ordination, Francis began to show signs of an extraordinary holiness, especially during the celebration of Holy Mass, which would normally last an hour and a half.

Due to a strange illness in which he experienced unusually high fevers, Padre Pio temporarily left his monastery of San Giovanni Rotondo to recover at home. On September 20, 1915, he felt stabbing and burning pains in both his hands and feet and on his left side under the heart. No mark was visible, but the pain was there nonetheless. Padre Pio had received the invisible stigmata, the bloodless, but painful wounds that matched the wounds of the Crucified Saviour.

In the Spring of 1916, one year after receiving the invisible stigmata, Padre Pio was drafted for military service. Because of poor health his induction was delayed, but he was finally declared fit and was assigned to the Medical Corps in Naples. Poor health recurred so that he was either in the hospital or at home convalesing. Finally, after less than a year in military service, Padre Pio was discharged.

Returning to San Giovanni Rotondo, he scrupulously fulfilled all the duties of the community while enduring both a mystical purgation of his soul as well as the pains of the invisible stigmata.

After offering Holy Mass on the morning of September 20, 1918, Padre Pio knelt in the church choir to make his thanksgiving. As was his custom, he knelt at the foot of a large crucifix. It was the third anniversary of his reception of the invisible stigmata. Suddenly, coming from the five wounds of the crucifix were five luminous rays that penetrated his hands, feet and side. The joy and the pain he experienced were so great that he swooned and fell to the floor. Padre Pio was the first priest to be blessed with the holy stigmata.

The wounds were repeatedly examined by doctors, one being Dr. Romanelli, who exclaimed that he "could not find a clinical symptom that could authorize me to classify those wounds." Nor could he explain scientifically why the wounds "do not fester, show no complications and do not heal."

Dr. Giorgio Festa noted that the wounds appeared clear and fresh, "with evident signs of a luminous radiation all along the borders." This was a phenomenon also reported by Dr. L. Romanelli.

After examining the wounds soon after their appearance, the provincial superior said, "If I were questioned by superior authority on this point, I would state, under oath (such is the certainty of the impression I have received), that looking through the wounds in the palms of Padre Pio's hands, one would have been able to see in all its details a piece of writing or another object placed on the opposite side of his hands."

Padre Pio was to experience mental suffering caused by suspicion, condemnation, criticism and claims that the wounds were produced by hysteria. He nevertheless performed all his duties in obedience and humility. Later, when his wounds were regarded as genuine, he endured numerous medical examinations and frequent visits from both the clergy and various laymen. He received countless pieces of mail and was overwhelmed at times by crowds that clamored for his attention.

The holy friar was to experience many mystical phenomena including the gift of prophecy, the reading of souls, visions, supernatural knowledge, bilocation and the odor of sanctity. He was frequently visited by angels and the souls in Purgatory who asked for his prayers. Many were the physical cures he performed and many were the converts he gave to the church. He was able to exorcize demons, but in turn the devil assaulted the holy friar on numerous occasions.

The Holy Masses offered by Padre Pio were most extraordinary, with the holy friar often lapsing into ecstasies which lengthened the Sacrifice to an hour and a half. Although the pain of the stigmata was almost always constant, the pains became more acute during the Holy Mass when fresh blood would appear on the hands. The monastery church was always crowded for the Holy Masses of Padre Pio. It was regarded as a profound spiritual favor not only to assist at the Padre's Masses, but also to receive the Holy Eucharist from his hands and to be blessed by him.

By the year 1966 Padre Pio had developed a serious heart condition and endured crushing pains in the chest. He also suffered severe attacks of asthma and bronchitis, arthritis and osteoporosis—all of this in addition to the pains of the stigmata.

Padre Pio died on September 23, 1968, after celebrating the golden jubilee of his reception of the visible stigmata. It is estimated that 100,000 people gathered at San Giovanni Rotondo for the funeral services.

The introduction of Padre Pio's cause for canonization was submitted the year following his death. In November, 1980, the cause received apostolic approval.

Countless devotees around the world look forward expectantly to the holy friar's eventual glorification as a canonized Saint of the Church.

A **CLOSE VIEW** of the Crucifix of Padre Pio. (See page 152).

PADRE PIO received the visible stigmata in 1918 while he prayed before this crucifix. He had received the invisible stigmata three years earlier.

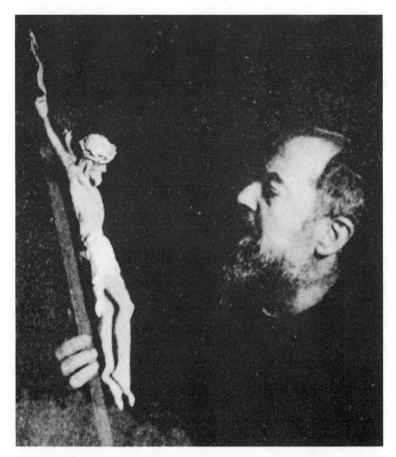

THE HOLY FRIAR Padre Pio received the gifts of prophecy, the reading of hearts, visions, supernatural knowledge, bilocation and miraculous perfume, as well as the ability to perform cures, exorcise demons and win converts miraculously. He frequently was visited by angels, but he was also assaulted by the devil on numerous occasions.

— 29 —

THE CRUCIFIX OF ST. PAUL OF THE CROSS

1694-1775

St. Paul of the Cross was born at Ovada in Piedmont, Italy, the son of devout parents. His childhood was distinguished by an incident in which he and his brother, John Baptist, fell into a river and were rescued by a beautiful lady whom they understood to be the Blessed Virgin. Devout from childhood, he progressively grew deeper in the spiritual life until, at the age of fifteen, he decided to devote his life to prayer and penance.

At the age of twenty he felt that duty required him to join the Venetian army to fight against the Turks in the defense of Christendom. This experience only proved to him that his vocation was elsewhere. After his discharge, he returned to his life of prayer.

After a series of visions in which he was directed to found a congregation that was to be especially devoted to the Passion, Paul composed a rule that was approved by Rome. Known as the Passionist Order, Paul and his brother, John Baptist, who had joined him, both settled on Monte Argentaro and there received the first novices. The austere life of the community also included the mission of preaching throughout the countryside, and it was this work that occupied most of the Saint's life.

St. Paul of the Cross possessed many of the mystical gifts including prophecy, bi-location, supernatural perfumes, visions, power over nature and levitation. Recognized as a Saint during his lifetime, he was usually met by throngs of people who were anxious to obtain a piece of his habit as a relic, to touch him or to request a cure or a favor.

The Saint also possessed extraordinary power over the devil. Once while giving a mission in Orbetello, there was a great commotion in the soldiers' barracks. One of the soldiers, screaming in terror, was being dragged and jostled by an invisible force. St. Paul was brought to the scene and with his crucifix held high, he commanded the spirit to depart. When the devil resisted, he ordered the soldier to make an act of contrition. The Saint then demanded the departure of the devil. No longer able to resist, the evil spirit left. The soldier confessed his sins and thereafter enjoyed peace of soul and mind.

The Saint's power over nature was exhibited on a number of occasions, especially at Santaflora, where he was to give a talk. Because of his great popularity, the church was crowded. An even greater number of people gathered in the square outside the church. So that both groups could hear him, the Saint stood at the church door and began to speak. The day was clear and bright, but suddenly the sky became dark and rain began to fall in torrents. The people immediately panicked and ran about in confusion. Seeing in this disturbance the work of the devil, the missionary held his crucifix high and blessed the air. Immediately the sky cleared and the people returned to their places. To the wonderment of all, everyone in the square was completely dry, whereas a moment before they had been thoroughly wet.

During another sermon to the people gathered outdoors, the sky suddenly became dark and threatened a terrible storm. Assuring his listeners that it was the work of the devil to prevent the good they were gaining, Paul blessed the black clouds with his crucifix. To the amazement of the people, the rain fell all around, but not a drop of water touched the Saint or the members of his audience.

In his biography of the Saint, Rev. Pius of the Name of Mary tells of a truly astounding miracle that took place when the Saint was scheduled to conduct a mission on the Isle of Elba and was in need of a ship to take him there. The Saint approached a sea captain, who indicated that his ship was badly damaged from a storm at sea and had been drawn up on shore. The Saint told the captain not to worry, that through the power of God their journey would be successful. Captain Fanciullo, an eyewitness, tells what took place.

> Wherefore the master, with his sailors and myself, began to haul the vessel towards the sea. The servant of God, too, taking his crucifix from his breast, held it up with his left hand, and with his right helped to haul. In an instant the vessel was in the sea, and both I and others standing by thought it a miracle to get it into the sea with so few hands. I saw Father Paul embark

and set sail for Porto Ferrajo, on the Isle of Elba, which they happily reached. News reached us that no sooner were they disembarked, than the vessel split in two and sank.

A miracle reminiscent of St. Anthony and the donkey adoring the Holy Eucharist took place while St. Paul of the Cross was walking beside a farmer who was driving his two young oxen. When the animals became agitated and began giving the farmer some trouble, he blasphemed so badly that the Saint began to admonish him. Becoming even angrier, the farmer leveled a gun at the Saint. Horrified more at the indecent language than he was frightened for his own life, the Saint drew his crucifix from his belt and held it high, saying: "Since you will not respect this crucifix, these oxen will." As if they understood, the oxen fell immediately to their knees before the image of the crucified Saviour. At the sight of the miracle, the farmer threw down his gun, begged pardon of the Saint and soon went to Confession and reconciled himself to God.

The most astounding miracle involving the Saint took place at Piagaro in the year 1738 during the course of a mission. At the end of the mission, the Saint repeated these words: "There are many here to whom it seems a thousand years before I end my mission (on earth), but I shall leave another behind, who will carry on the mission better than I." When the Saint left the church some of the people followed him, while the rest remained in the church to pray. Rev. Pius of the Name of Mary tells us that:

> All of a sudden, they were astounded at seeing a blue sweat beginning to flow in great abundance from a large crucifix of wood, which is preserved in that church. The priests brought cloths to receive the sacred liquor, while some of the people, recollecting what the holy missionary had said, ran to tell him what had happened. He made no reply but this, "I knew it already." He then asked of what color was the sweat, and being told it was blue, he added: "It is a good sign," and then went on with his journey. The effect was what he had expected. Those who had not been moved by the thunder of his voice, were brought to repentance by the

sight of the miracle. For a perpetual remembrance of this wonderful event, a new chapel was built, in which the miraculous image was placed, with an appropriate inscription, as may be seen to this day.

St. Paul of the Cross died at the age of 80 and was canonized in 1867.

ST. PAUL OF THE CROSS

THE CRUCIFIX of St. Paul of the Cross.

DEVOUT FROM CHILDHOOD, St. Paul of the Cross performed various miracles with the crucifix held high.

30

THE CRUCIFIX OF ST. PEREGRINE LAZIOSI

1265-1345

Born in Forli, Italy, Peregrine was taught the ways of prayer by his devout mother, but instead of being influenced by her, he preferred to devote his time to athletic endeavors and won the acceptance of his peers by indulging his impetuous nature. When St. Philip Benizi was preaching in the public square, Peregrine displayed his contempt by striking the Saint soundly in the face. The Saint prayed for Peregrine's return to virtue, and some years later, through the workings of grace, St. Philip Benizi welcomed Peregrine into the Servite Order at Siena.

The number of persons Peregrine converted to the Faith was outstanding, his work among penitents and sinners was extensive, his travels on errands of mercy were numerous and his miracles were countless.

When Peregrine was about 60 years of age he was stricken with a cancer of the leg that pained him, but did not interrupt his works of mercy nor his customary exercises of virtue. Eventually, when gangrene consumed the flesh of his leg to the bone, the amputation of the leg was recommended as the only means of preserving his life.

On the eve of the operation, St. Peregrine visited the chapter room of the monastery to pray before a painting that depicts the Crucifixion. We are told that he remained praying there throughout most of the night. After Peregrine had been praying for many hours, the picture became animated. Christ stretched His hand from the painting and touched the Saint's diseased leg, which was later found to be completely healed with no trace of the former ailment. The renowned surgeon who was scheduled to perform the amputation, arrived the next morning for the operation and promptly acknowledged the miraculous nature of the cure. Because of this miracle, countless victims of cancer devoutly pray to St. Peregrine for the cure of their disease.

THE MIRACULOUS CRUCIFIX PAINTING of St. Peregrine Laziosi (1265-1345). St. Peregrine prayed before this painting throughout most of the night preceding the scheduled amputation of his leg. The picture became animated, Our Lord reaching out and miraculously healing the cancerous leg.

THE CHAPTER ROOM that contains the miraculous painting through which St. Peregrine was healed about the year 1325.

THE HEALING of St. Peregrine is recreated in this painting.

31

THE CRUCIFIX OF ST. RITA OF CASCIA

1381-1457

In obedience to her elderly parents, but against her natural incli-nations, Rita was married to Paolo Ferdinando when she was only 12 years of age. The marriage proved to be an unhappy one. Rita had much to suffer from a husband who was described as being "rough, ill-tempered, and profligate." Shortly before his politically motivated assassination, Paolo's disposition was completely trans-formed and for a time the household was an ideal one, a fact credited to Rita's patience and constant prayers.

When Rita's two sons came of age a serious trial was presented when they vowed to avenge their father's death. When Rita's entreaties and prayers failed to change their plans, she prayed for their deaths rather than have them commit the sin of murder. In due time her prayers were answered when both sons died after forgiving their father's murderers and receiving the consolations of the Church.

Shortly after the death of her sons, Rita applied for entrance into the convent of the Augustinians in Cascia, an order to which she had been attracted before her marriage. Her repeated requests to be admitted were denied due to a stipulation in the rule of the Order which barred the acceptance of widows. Turning to her favorite Saints, Augustine, Nicholas of Tolentino and John the Baptist, she appealed for help. Again her prayers were answered when the three Saints appeared to her one night and accompanied her to the Augustinian convent of Santa Maria Maddalena. Bolted gates and locked doors were miraculously opened to permit her entrance into the chapel. When the astonished nuns discovered her the next morn-ing they realized that her unusual entry was the holy will of God and accepted her as a member of their order. Many years later the same convent would be renamed in Rita's honor.

After hearing a sermon preached by St. James of the Marches, Rita was inspired to ask God for some participation in Christ's sufferings. Still another prayer was answered while she was kneeling one day before a crucifix that had been painted on the wall of the oratory. While Rita was in deep prayer a luminous ray suddenly streaked from the crown of the Crucified, carrying with it a pointed thorn. This fixed itself on the forehead of Rita with such force that it penetrated the bone. Unable at first to bear the torment, the Saint fell in a swoon.

The wound eventually festered and produced such an offensive odor that the next 15 years of the Saint's life were spent in virtual seclusion.

There was one brief interruption to her sufferings. During the Holy Year of 1450, members of the community prepared to pilgrimage to Rome to gain the plenary indulgence. Because of the infected wound that was additionally contaminated with worms, Rita was denied permission to join them. After St. Rita's fervent prayer, however, the wound disappeared. Rita was then permitted to join her companions, but upon her return to the convent the wound promptly reappeared.

Three days before her death, at the age of 76, Rita was blessed with a vision of Our Lord and His holy Mother. At the time of St. Rita's entrance into Heaven, the cell in which she lay was filled with an extraordinary perfume, while a light emanated from the wound on her forehead. The bells of the city are said to have been joyously pealed by angels.

Many phenomena have been reported both during the Saint's life and after her death. One of the most extraordinary is the presence of her incorrupt body, which lies exposed in a crystal casket in the church at Cascia which was built in her honor.

St. Rita has taken her rightful position among the great Saints who served in turn as wives, mothers, widows and nuns who were providentially given to us for our edification. The Saint is overwhelmingly and affectionately regarded by her many satisfied devotees around the world as the Patron Saint of Desperate and Impossible Cases.

THE CRUCIFIX OF ST. RITA of Cascia (1381-1457), painted on the wall of the church oratory where St. Rita was praying on her knees at the time her forehead was penetrated by a luminous ray which issued from the crucifix.

"SAINT OF THE IMPOSSIBLE," St. Rita is the Patron Saint of desperate and "impossible" cases.

A GREAT YEARNING to participate in Our Lord's sufferings sprang up in St. Rita after she heard a sermon preached by St. James of the Marches. She was soon favored by the event artistically shown here.

ST. RITA, in another illustration of the miraculous wound she received while praying before an image of Our Lord's Crucifixion.

THE CRUCIFIX OF ST. THOMAS AQUINAS

1225-1274

Thomas' family was one of great distinction. His father, Landulph, was Count of Aquino; Theodora, his mother, was Countess of Teano. In addition, his family was related to the Emperors Henry VI and Frederick II and to the Kings of Aragon, Castile and France.

Before his birth a holy hermit allegedly foretold his career, telling Theodora that her son would "enter the Order of Friars Preachers, and so great will be his learning and sanctity that in his day no one will be found to equal him."

In compliance with the prevailing custom of the time for members of distinguished families, Thomas was sent at the age of five to be trained by the Benedictine monks at Monte Cassino. He was diligent in study and was already devoted to meditation and prayer. After leaving this famed abbey he was sent to Naples, where he received additional training in what was then known as "the seven liberals."

After receiving advice from John of St. Julian, a noted preacher of the time, Thomas received the habit of the Order of St. Dominic. His entrance surprised almost everyone, who wondered why a young man of such potential and family position should reject a brilliant secular career for one of poverty and penance.

Theodora, Thomas' mother, was likewise surprised and devised a plan to have his brothers abduct him. While Thomas was confined in the fortress of San Giovanni, his brothers and sisters endeavored by various means to destroy his vocation. The brothers even laid a snare one night to destroy his virtue by introducing a harlot into his room. The Saint is said to have driven her from the chamber with a hot poker from the fireplace. His mother finally agreed to his release after Thomas had spent two years in confinement.

Sent once more for additional studies, he was placed under Albertus Magnus, the most renowned professor of the Order. It is reported that Thomas' humility and silence during his early years of study were sometimes misinterpreted by his professors and fellow students so that he was often called "the dumb ox." Albertus Magnus, however, once exclaimed after hearing Thomas defend a difficult thesis, "We call this young man a dumb ox, but his bellowing in doctrine will one day resound throughout the world."

Ordained a priest in 1250, his sermons are said to have been "forceful, redolent of piety, full of solid instruction, and abounding in apt citations from Scripture." Sometime after his ordination he received the degree of Doctor of Theology on the same day as did his friend, St. Bonaventure. From this time on St. Thomas' life may be summed up in a few words: praying, preaching, teaching, writing and journeying. His counsels were sought by both the faithful and the scholar, while his company was often requested by the Pope.

A description of the Saint as he appeared in life is given by Calo, who tells that "his features corresponded with the greatness of his soul. He was of lofty stature and of heavy build, but straight and well-proportioned. His complexion was like the colour of new wheat. His head was large and well-shaped, and he was slightly bald."

St. Thomas is the author of the beautiful Office of Corpus Christi, and the words to the benediction hymns *Tantum Ergo* and *O Salutaris Hostia*.

Although the Saint lived less than 50 years, he composed more than 60 works, some of great length. Of these, the most famous are the *Summa Contra Gentiles,* a manual and systematic defense of Christian doctrine, and the *Summa Theologica,* an exposition of theology on philosophical principles. Historians tell us that the Saint had the ability to dictate to several scribes at the same time.

His biographers relate that he was often found in ecstasy. On one occasion at Naples in 1273, after completing his treatise on the Holy Eucharist, his brethren found him in ecstasy before a crucifix and heard a voice coming from the image of the Crucified saying: "Thou hast written well of Me, Thomas; what reward wilt thou have?" To which Thomas replied, "None other than Thyself, Lord."

St. Thomas was a philosopher and theologian and is regarded as a luminary of dogmatic theology. He was called *Doctor Communis, Doctor Angelicus* and The Great Synthesizer. Since the year 1567 he has also been known as a Doctor of the Church, and in 1880 he was named the patron of Catholic schools and education.

PATRON of Catholic schools and of education, St. Thomas Aquinas.

IN ECSTASY before a crucifix, St. Thomas Aquinas heard a voice coming from the image.

ST. THOMAS AQUINAS and the other Doctors of the Church.

33

THE CRUCIFIX OF
ST. THOMAS OF VILLANOVA

1488-1555

Regarded as the glory of the church of Spain, St. Thomas was the son of devout parents, his father being a miller of modest means. At the age of sixteen he was sent to the University of Alcala, where he completed his studies with great success. Ten years later he was made professor of philosophy. After teaching for two years he was offered the chair of philosophy at the University of Salamanca, but he declined the post and instead joined the Augustinian friars. After ordination he served as prior at Salamanca, Burgos and Valladolid and was twice elected provincial.

He fell into frequent raptures especially at Mass. Afterwards his face shone like that of Moses, dazzling the eyes of those who saw him. Emperor Charles V nominated the Saint to the archbishopric of Valencia, which Thomas declined; but he eventually accepted under holy obedience. Always a lover of poverty, St. Thomas traveled to his new assignment on foot while wearing the old monastic habit and hat he had worn since his profession. As archbishop he was particularly mindful of orphans, the poor, sinners and captives and is known to have spent many nights in prayer for the conversion of notorious sinners.

Thomas would often say, "I was never so much afraid of being excluded from the number of the elect as since I have been a bishop." For this reason Thomas more than once asked for permission to resign and often consulted his confessor on the matter. On the day of the Purification, February 2, while Thomas was praying in his oratory, a voice coming from his crucifix said to him, "Thomas, afflict not yourself, but be patient. On the day of My Mother's nativity [September 8] you shall receive the recompense of all your troubles."

As an incontestable proof of this revelation, the mouth of the crucifix, which before had sweated blood in his sight, now remained open, although it had previously been closed. The Bollandists in their Acta Sanctorum under the date September 8 report what was more surprising still: the mouth of the Saviour now had a perfect set of teeth made of copper.

In August of 1555, St. Thomas experienced heart problems which grew in severity until, on September 8, the birthday of Our Lady and the day indicated in the revelation, he died peacefully, being then in the sixty-seventh year of his age and the eleventh of his episcopal dignity.

ST. THOMAS OF VILLANOVA (1488-1555), depicted in a portrait by Juan de Juanes. The facial image was taken from an impression made by the artist prior to burial of the Saint. The portrait is located in the cathedral of Valencia, Spain. When the humble St. Thomas wanted to resign as bishop, he was answered from his crucifix. (Photo courtesy of Augustinian Press).

34

THE CRUCIFIX OF
ST. VERONICA GIULIANI

d. 1727

When Veronica's mother was dying, she entrusted each of her five children to a sacred wound of Christ. Veronica, then four years old and the youngest, was assigned the wound in the side. This action of the dying mother might well have been prophetic, because her daughter's interest in the Passion grew to become an intense devotion.

When Veronica recognized her vocation to the religious life and expressed a desire to enter the Capuchin Monastery at Citta di Castello, her father refused his permission. Due to Veronica's insistent pleadings, however, he eventually weakened and permitted her to leave. Under the primitive rule of St. Clare, Veronica quickly advanced in virtue, which was rewarded with revelations, ecstasies and numerous visions of the suffering Christ. After one of her visions in which she accepted the chalice of Our Lord's sufferings, she experienced some of the sufferings in her own body and soul. Later the five sacred wounds were visibly impressed upon her on Good Friday in the year 1697.

By order of the Holy See, the bishop of the diocese put the phenomenon to a thorough test. Veronica was not only isolated from the rest of her community, but she also submitted to constant supervision and was denied the reception of the Holy Eucharist. Special gloves bearing the bishop's signet were placed on her hands, and medical treatments were conducted.

According to sworn testimony in the Process for Veronica's beatification, her confessor and her fellow religious testified that the stigmatic wounds opened and bled at command, and further, that the wounds closed and healed in a brief time in the presence of the bishop. Eventually Veronica's humble demeanor, patience and obedience proved to her skeptical associates and contemporaries that her mystical gifts and stigmatic wounds were authentic.

St. Veronica Giuliani was a woman of great common sense and administrative ability, in addition to having been endowed with many supernatural favors. Her judgments were highly respected, since she served the community as novice mistress for 34 years and held the office of abbess for 11 years. In her diary, written at the command of her confessor, she left an invaluable record which was used during the Process of her beatification and which has proved to be of great interest to theologians. Her works include 44 volumes, containing by far a most intriguing account of mystical phenomena.

Apoplexy severely troubled the Saint as she approached the end of her life. She died of the complications on July 9, 1727, and she was canonized in 1839.

St. Veronica's body remained incorrupt for many years, until it was destroyed by an inundation of the Tiber River. The heart of the Saint, removed soon after her death, bore for many years distinct symbols of the Passion which corresponded exactly to drawings made by the Saint shortly before her death. The heart is kept in a special reliquary and is said by physicians to be well preserved. In recent years, though, the figures have become less defined.

A death mask clearly indicating the Saint's features has been carefully maintained, as have her cell, her bed and a number of mementoes.

Also kept is a crucifix that is of particular interest. One day, this venerated image became animated. Turning toward the Saint, it began to cry and drip blood. The Crucified then invited Veronica to embrace and kiss the wound through which the Divine Heart had been pierced. The wound, He said, confirmed His willingness to pardon sinners and was the conduit through which He dispensed the merits of His Passion. This brings to mind the incident in the Saint's childhood when her dying mother entrusted Veronica to the wound in the side of the Crucified Saviour.

THE MIRACULOUS CRUCIFIX of St. Veronica Giuliani, which became animated and then turned toward the Saint. The image of Our Lord wept, bled and invited her to kiss the wound through which the Divine Heart had been pierced.

SUPERNATURAL FAVORS and practical abilities marked the life of St. Veronica Giuliani. She wrote 44 volumes, comprising intriguing accounts of mystical phenomena.

STIGMATIST AND VISIONARY, St. Veronica Giuliani is represented (above) in loving discourse with the Crucified Saviour, and kneeling before the Crucifix (at bottom of page).

THE SYMBOLS OF THE PASSION were found on the heart of St. Veronica Giuliani, which was extracted soon after her death. The marks corresponded exactly to drawings she had made shortly before she died.

THE CRUCIFIX OF ST. VINCENT FERRER

1350-1419

Born in Valencia, Spain, Vincent was educated in that city and, because of a keen intellect, he completed his studies at the age of 14. The Dominicans accepted him into their order in 1367, when he was 17 years old. Four years later he was teaching philosophy.

During a critical illness that threatened his life, St. Vincent experienced a marvelous vision of St. Francis and St. Dominic, who encouraged him to embark on a mission of preaching penance and conversion. Miraculously cured, Vincent was supported by this vision and obtained the Pope's blessing before setting out on missionary travels that would occupy the next 20 years of his life.

Wandering through Spain, France, Switzerland and Italy, Vincent touched the souls of countless listeners. Especially influenced by his preaching were St. Margaret of Savoy and St. Bernardine of Siena, who gained many converts to the Faith in his native Italy.

Although Vincent spoke only Limousin, the language of Valencia, he was understood by listeners of many different nationalities. Contemporary biographers reported that Vincent possessed the gift of tongues, a view that was also supported by Nicholas Clemangis of the University of Paris, who was a witness to the phenomenon.

Vincent's preachings were punctuated with miraculous cures, which also gave rise to numerous conversions. Vincent's first biographer, Peter Razzano, estimated that 25,000 Jews were won to the Faith, as were thousands of Moors. St. Vincent is remembered as having told his listeners, "I am the Angel of the Judgment."

Together with St. Colette, he is credited with ending the Western Schism when three popes claimed the chair of Peter. After some difficulty, he persuaded them to resign. The Council of Constance then met in 1414 to elect Martin V.

While journeying through Europe, St. Vincent always carried a tall wooden cross which he used as a staff and which he either planted in the ground or stood in the pulpit beside him when he preached. After being told by St. Colette that he would die within two years—information she had learned during an ecstasy—he perhaps felt he had little need for his mission cross and gave it to her. This *"le baton de Maitre Vincent"* has a corpus that is tied to the cross with string. It is kept as a priceless relic at Besançon above the main altar. It was this cross that the Saint touched to the dead whom he commanded to rise in the name of Christ Crucified, and it was this cross which he held high before those to whom he preached in great cathedrals or on the open plains.

One night while looking upon the crucifix, St. Vincent was considering the sorrows of Jesus when he exclaimed, "O my Saviour, how great were Thy sufferings on the Cross!" His biographer, Fr. Teoli, relates that the crucifix turned its head toward the Saint on its right side and replied, "Yes, Vincent, I suffered all you say, and more, much more." The head of the corpus has retained the same position.

The two predictions of St. Colette were realized when St. Vincent Ferrer died two years later, not in his native Spain, but in France.

A MOST POWERFUL PREACHER, St. Vincent Ferrer (1350-1419) called
sinners to repentance. He is pictured here preaching to the Moors. St. Vincent spoke out so penetratingly that men, women and children fell to the
ground and pleaded with Heaven for mercy.

THE MISSION CRUCIFIX carried by St. Vincent Ferrer on his journeys through Europe. The wooden cross was sometimes used as a staff, and at other times was planted in the ground or stood in the pulpit beside him when he preached. The crucifix is taller than it appears in this picture.

ST. VINCENT FERRER'S mission cross has a corpus that is tied to the cross with a string. The miraculous crucifix was given to St. Colette after she predicted St. Vincent's imminent death. The priceless relic is now kept on the altar of the Monastery of St. Clare in Besançon, France.

"**WHATEVER YOU DO,** think not of yourselves but of God." This was the favorite saying of St. Vincent Ferrer, who was instrumental in settling a dispute over the papacy. One of the greatest saints of the Church, he converted thousands of souls and performed countless miracles.

—PART IV—

OTHER MIRACULOUS
IMAGES OF OUR LORD

— 36 —

THE HOLY SHROUD

Turin, Italy
33 A.D.

The Holy Shroud of Turin, which is imprinted with the full-length image of a crucified man, is one of the most mysterious, scientifically challenging and controversial relics of the Catholic Church. It has been regarded as the burial shroud of Jesus Christ from the earliest days, with its existence being connected to that of a cloth called the Edessan Image, or the Mandylion, which was also greatly revered.

The Shroud is believed to be the one mentioned in St. Luke's Gospel: "But Peter rising up, ran to the sepulchre, and stooping down, he saw the linen cloths laid by themselves; and went away wondering to himself at that which was come to pass." (*Luke* 23:12). St. John likewise mentions the Shroud in this manner: "Then cometh Simon Peter following him, and went into the sepulchre, and saw the linen cloths lying. And the napkin that had been about his head, not lying with the linen cloths, but apart, wrapped up into one place." (*John* 20:6-7). The "napkin" that was about His head was a cloth routinely used in Jewish burials to keep the jaw in place. Positioned under the chin, it was brought upward around the ears and was secured at the top of the head. It did not cover the face.

The transfer of the Shroud from Jerusalem to Edessa, now known as Urfa in eastern Turkey, was accomplished by Thaddaeus, "one of the seventy," who helped in the evangelization of that country. When Man'nu Vi was tormenting Christians, the cloth was hidden for safekeeping in a niche above Edessa's west gate. It remained there in a space which was hermetically sealed until its rediscovery in 525 when the wall was being rebuilt following a disastrous flood. It was identified without dispute as the original Image of Edessa and was confirmed as such by Emperor Justinian, who built the magnificent Hagia Sophia Cathedral in Constantinople for its safekeeping.

In time the Image of Edessa also became known as the Holy Mandylion, an Arabic word meaning veil or handkerchief. Since the Shroud is 14 feet long and three and a half feet wide, how could it have been called a veil or handkerchief? In order to disguise the Shroud, which would have been considered unclean and a thing to be avoided according to Jewish law, the Shroud was folded so that only the face was exposed. This theory is supported by recent photographs which indicate the folds, and also by a team of researchers which reconstructed the pattern of eight folds.

Ancient images of Christ were apparently based on the Shroud—particularly Byzantine icons, according to researchers who have conducted exhaustive comparisons. These researchers have developed evidence that the Shroud was known as early as the 6th century since Byzantine frescoes, paintings and mosaics of that century contain similarities that are peculiar to the Shroud image.

The Mandylion was sent on various travels about the year 944. For the first time since its removal from Jerusalem, the Mandylion was unfolded to reveal the complete image. Just as art was influenced by the face on the Shroud, from this time on lamentation scenes changed from the dead Christ wrapped mummy style to those which show Christ reclining in death in the attitude consistent with that on the Shroud.

Devotional exhibitions in various cities were conducted until the year 1204, when the image disappeared for almost 150 years. Historians believe this resulted from the misdirected zeal of the soldiers of the Fourth Crusade who, for reasons unknown, turned their attention from combatting infidels to aiming fury on Constantinople. Church treasures were stolen and buildings were destroyed.

It is believed that the Mandylion came into the possession of the Knights Templar, a group of righteous knights whose purpose was to defend Crusader territories. It is known that during their initiation rites a mysterious image of a head was honored. Members took vows of poverty, chastity and absolute obedience. Because their honesty was unquestioned they were entrusted with valuables, including relics and other valuable objects of devotion. It is certain that had they come into the possession of the Mandylion, they would have honored and defended it.

Geoffrey de Charny, one of the Knights Templar, emerged in the year 1350 as owner of the Mandylion. Following his death, his widow, struggling under the weight of financial difficulties, exhibited the relic for monetary gain. The bishop discontinued the exhibition which took place in the small French village of Lirey, a place 100 miles southeast of Paris. This exhibition nevertheless brought the Mandylion into prominence and established it as a very ancient devotional object.

Following the death of the widow, the relic became the property of Geoffrey de Charny II who, like his father, also left his widow in financial straits. After searching for a proper and secure situation for the relic, Margaret de Charny deeded it in 1453 to Louis of Savoy, perhaps with an exchange of money. (The House of Savoy owned the relic until 1983, when Italy's last king, exiled Umberto II of the House of Savoy, bequeathed it to the Vatican.)

A few years later, in 1464, Pope Sixtus IV let it be known that he believed in the authenticity of the Shroud.

An unfortunate accident took place on December 4, 1532 during a fire in the chapel at Chambery, France. Intense heat melted parts of the silver chest in which the Shroud was kept, causing molten silver to drip, scorch and burn the contents. Two Franciscan priests saved the relic when they carried its casket to safety and doused it with water. The image was not altered and was only slightly touched, although the cloth bears scorch marks, water stains and small holes that were caused by the molten silver. Larger holes made by the molten silver were repaired by Poor Clare nuns who applied 14 large triangular-shaped patches and eight smaller ones to repair the holes and to secure these areas to the rest of the fabric. The scorch marks proved to be advantageous since they provided scientists in recent times with opportunities to test various theories of how the image was formed.

Three saints are known to have gazed upon the relic. Forty-six years after the fire, the Shroud was taken to Turin, Italy for an exhibition. The relic was apparently well respected, since St. Charles Borromeo journeyed on foot from Milan to view it. During the exhibition of 1613, St. Francis de Sales served as one of the assistant bishops who held the cloth before the people. St. Jane Frances de Chantal, who assisted St. Francis de Sales in founding the Order of the Visitation, venerated the Shroud during another exposition in 1639.

A permanent home for the relic was established in the Royal Chapel of the Turin Cathedral in 1694. It is here that the Shroud is found today, enshrined in a splendid manner.

The most dramatic event in the Shroud's history is unquestionably that which took place during the exhibition of 1898, when it was photographed for the first time. Photography was then only 30 years old and still in an experimental state when the Shroud was photographed by Secondo Pia, then a 43-year-old counselor and attorney who had also won several awards as an amateur photographer. With electric lighting then new and uncertain, Pia nevertheless used this illumination to photograph the Shroud at night as it was kept under a glass covering. The first exposure of 14 minutes was followed by another of 20 minutes. Pia retired to his darkroom to develop the plates around midnight. For the rest of his life Pia would recount the emotions he experienced when the image formed in the developing pan under his gaze. Pia tells us: "Shut up in my darkness, all intent on my work, I experienced a very strong emotion when, during the development, I saw for the first time the Holy Face appear on the plate with such clarity that I was dumbfounded by it."

Pia's image was a positive print, an historic discovery which revealed for the first time that the image on the ancient cloth was a negative, a photographic representation that was unknown until the late 19th century.

Secondo Pia's cumbersome, wooden, boxlike camera that was used in this magnificent discovery is kept in the Holy Shroud Museum in Turin.

The Shroud attracted the scientific curiosity of many distinguished men of science, among them Dr. Pierre Barbet, an eminent French surgeon, who has given us a detailed study of the wounds in his book, *A Doctor at Calvary*. Another medical man, Yves Delage, a professor of anatomy at the Sorbonne and an acknowledged agnostic, gave a detailed study in 1902 in which he concluded that the Man of the Shroud was none other than Jesus Christ.

Both physicians noted that the body was of a man accustomed to hard labor, well built and muscular. All the wounds proved to be anatomically correct, and while the body showed definite signs of rigor mortis, there was no evidence of decay. Their studies show that under conditions in which He was buried, severe bodily decomposition would normally occur in the Middle East within three to four days.

Together with other men of science, they noted that the face is covered with bruises. Swellings appear about both eyes, both cheeks and the chin. A fracture of the nose is possible. Around and atop the head are wounds which indicate that the Crown of Thorns was really in the shape of a cap.

The wound made in the heart by the lance was measured at one and three quarters of an inch by seven-sixteenths of an inch and was made after death, since the flow dribbled down. Had the victim been alive at the time, the blood and water would have spurted out by the contraction of the heart.

Originating from the left wrist are two flows of blood which indicate an important feature since they measure at approximately 10 degrees apart. This establishes the fact that the victim assumed two positions on the cross. With the body hanging full weight from the nails in the wrists, the muscles of the chest were stretched to the extreme. This caused the victim double pain in the wrists, combined with the difficulty in breathing. The victim was therefore forced to repeatedly exchange this difficulty for another pain since the victim had to actually stand on the nail that pierced both feet to relieve the pressure for breathing.

The distended abdomen indicates asphyxiation, the essential aspect of crucifixion, since the muscles of the chest become paralyzed from the position of the body in the hanging attitude.

Both knees are bruised and cut, particularly the left one. Bruises and abrasions are also found on the upper back indicating that a heavy object was carried, but only after the scourging, since the marks of the scourging in that area were altered by this larger wound.

The wounds of the scourging have been numbered by one examiner as being between 90 and 120. Another counted 200 wounds. Both agree that the wounds were produced by a dumbbell-shaped instrument identical in size and shape to the Roman flagrum. It was apparent to these examiners that two men inflicted the wounds, the one on the right being taller, more aggressive and sadistic than his companion on the left.

Photographs of the Shroud were taken for a second time during an exhibition in 1931. Present was septuagenarian Secondo Pia. The photographer at this event was Commander Giuseppe Enrie, who took a dozen photos of the precious relic. Of superb quality, these prints are still reproduced today from the glass plates that he used.

In attendance at this 1931 exhibition was a young priest, the future Pope Paul VI.

The holy relic was enshrined in peace until October 1, 1972 when a deliberate attempt was made to destroy it by fire. The perpetrator remains unknown, but because of the asbestos inside the reliquary, his efforts were unsuccessful and the Shroud survived.

During the first televised exposition of the Shroud the year following this attempt, Pope Paul VI recalled his emotions when he saw the Shroud at the 1931 exposition: "It appears so true, so profound, so human and so divine, such as we have been unable to admire and venerate in any other image."

During the same year as this televised exhibition, 1973, the Shroud was studied by Gilbert Raes, a professor at Ghent Institute of Textile Technology in Belgium. He determined that the cloth is made of linen, a textile derived from flax. He observed traces of cotton among the linen fibers, an indication that the cloth had been woven on a loom that had been used for weaving cotton. The Middle East origins of the Shroud were supported by the presence of cotton, since cotton was grown in the Middle East in apostolic times but was not grown in Europe. He also reported that the weave of the cloth, a herringbone pattern, was a type common in the Middle East in the first century. His findings are in accord with the opinion of Silvio Curto, associate professor of Egyptology at the University of Turin, who declared that the fabric could indeed date to the time of Christ.

A Swiss criminologist, Max Frei, was asked during the same year, 1973, to authenticate certain features of the Shroud. A botanist by training, he noticed pollen spores on the cloth and was permitted to take samples for examination and classification. These proved to be samples of 49 different plants. Thirty-three specimens were from plants grown in Palestine, Istanbul and from the southern steppes of Turkey. Sixteen of the plants had European origins and probably had attached themselves to the cloth during open-air exhibition in France and later showings in Italy. It is known that the Shroud never left Europe after its display in Lirey in 1357. These findings of Max Frei support the Mandylion-Shroud theory.

The most thorough and scientifically probing examination of the Shroud was made by a group of 20 highly qualified scientists from the United States known as the Shroud of Turin Research Project.

The team arrived in Italy in October of 1978 with their scientific instruments packed in 72 crates. Their examination of the Shroud is regarded as the most extensive study of an ancient artifact ever conducted.

Among the scientists were a pathologist, a medical school professor, image-enhancement specialists, physicists, physical chemists, spectroscopy experts, archeologists, thermography and microanalysts and X-ray specialists. Only two of the scientists had studied the Shroud previously. Most came with the expectation that their tests would reveal the Shroud to be a forgery. The tests performed over a five-day period only deepened the mystery of the Shroud, so much so that it took three years for numerous scientists in the United States and Europe to draw conclusions.

The scientists were permitted to handle the cloth and were surprised to find it light and silky to the touch, ivory colored with age, clean looking, and having a damask-like surface sheen. For the most part it was woven in a single piece, except for a strip approximately three and a half inches wide which was joined by a single seam that ran along the length of the left side.

The scientists described the image as having a sepia monochrome tint which clearly shows the front and back views of a powerfully built man in an attitude of death. The closer one looks at the image, the more it seems to dissolve in a mist, a curiosity which indicates that the features are only distinguishable at a distance, while photographs seem to enhance its details.

It was found that the image does not penetrate the cloth, but affects only the topmost fibers of each thread with a yellow discoloration extending only two or three fibers into the thread structure. The darker areas are not a deeper yellow, but only appear darker because they contain more discolored fibers than the lighter areas.

Their photos of the Shroud reveal that the victim was between 30 and 35 years of age, measured approximately 5'11" in height and weighed approximately 175 pounds. A former Harvard professor who specialized in ethnology observed that the height of the man is consistent with Jewish grave findings of the first century, the average male measuring approximately 5'10". The victim's beard, hair and facial features are consistent with a Jewish or Semitic facial grouping, according to the Smithsonian Museum of Natural Sciences. The museum also notes that the facial features match those of modern-day Arabs of noble rank, or sephardic Jews.

The body is clearly unwashed and naked. We are told in Scripture that Jesus died on the eve of the Passover Sabbath, a day of special solemnity. Various delays after the death at three o'clock caused a postponement of the body's anointing. Joseph of Arimathea had to gain an audience with Pilate to ask for the body, documents had to be drawn, the death confirmed, a burial linen had to be purchased, and the body removed from the Cross and carried to the tomb. According to Jewish law a body had to be removed by sundown and all work terminated at six o'clock. For these reasons the body of Jesus was consigned to the tomb hurriedly without the usual washing and ceremonial anointing. We also learn from Scripture that the anointing was never accomplished since the women who arrived at the tomb on Easter morning to perform this ceremony on the body found the tomb empty.

Tests revealed that the image is that of a real corpse. Using a process called isodensity, it was found that there were three-dimensional properties on the Shroud which appeared to such perfection that a model of the body was fashioned from it. This process also revealed that the unnatural bulges on the eyes were actually coins having 24 features which matched a coin issued by Pontius Pilate between A.D. 29 and 32 known as a lepton.

The back of the Shroud was examined for the first time in 400 years. The theory that the image penetrates only the topmost fibers of the threads was confirmed, since no trace of the image could be found on the back of the cloth.

That the image was an impression made by contact with a statue or an actual body was explored and considered, but all contact impressions made by the scientists proved to be improperly shaded and distorted. These impressions made by the scientists were neither superficial or three-dimensional. The theory was rejected, since the man of the shroud was lying on his back with the body pressing heavily against the cloth, whereas only the weight of the cloth came in contact with the top of the body, thus producing unequal pressures that made it impossible to duplicate. The scientists found that the body had not been moved, unwrapped or rewrapped, and that the cloth had to be removed other than by natural means, since blood clots would have smeared or been broken, especially at the back area where maximum pressure existed.

Also discounted was the suggestion that the image was formed by vapors from the body, such as from sweat, blood, burial spices, ammonia or urea. It was declared obvious that vapors diffusing from a body through space cannot be that exact, since they do not necessarily travel upward in an orderly manner, but diffuse randomly into the air.

The scorch theory was confirmed by the team. Since the scorch areas caused by the fire of 1532 were so close to the image, a resemblance was noted. Three tests were employed, these being fluorescence, infrared spectroscopy and spectrometry, to confirm the theory that the image was caused by heat or light applied in a gradual manner.

Examined very thoroughly were the blood marks which were found to contain iron oxide, protein and porphryin, all components of human blood.

Emphatically dismissed was the supposition that the image was a painting. A professor of biology at the Institut Catholique in Paris, Paul Vignon, exclaimed, "No painter, in his most elaborate work, has ever risen to such exactitude." It was declared that no ancient or medieval artist could have produced a work with such anatomical, pathological and medical expertise. An artist would have had extreme difficulty in checking the progress of his work since the image can barely be seen up close and can only be discerned at a distance of from 15 to 20 feet. Moreover, the history of the Shroud can be traced to the Middle Ages, when the concept of negativity in photography was unknown. It was also questioned why a forger in the Middle Ages would have painted the image in negative form when his work would not have been appreciated for approximately 500 years, when the principles of photography were discovered.

The team of researchers also proved, by employing a battery of elaborate tests, that not only is the image three-dimensional and superficial, but it is also non-directional, that is, no brush strokes or signs of a directional pattern were found, such as would have been noted had the image been painted by hand. The only direction found was the pattern of the cloth itself. Additionally, there were no traces of a medium, pigments, stains, oils, powders, dyes or inks. The definite conclusion was that the image was not produced by an artist.

It was found that the yellow coloration of the image is chemically stable and cannot be changed by chemical agents, nor can it be dissolved or bleached. It was also found that the image remained unaffected by the dousing with water received during the 1532 fire.

Efforts to duplicate the image using modern technology proved unsuccessful, leading one authority to declare, "The image is a mystery."

While many popes and ecclesiastics have expressed the opinion that the image of the Shroud is that of Jesus Christ, the Roman Catholic Church has never declared this opinion in an official manner. Members of the research team avoided identifying the image as that of Jesus, although a number of its members have independently and publicly voiced the belief that it is. The physical, historical and chemical features of the Shroud advance strong evidence for the victim's resurrection and they have pointed out various aspects recorded in Scripture that are present on the Shroud, but which were not present in a normal crucifixion in the time of Christ. These unusual features include the scourging, the crowning with thorns, the absence of broken leg bones, the postmortem wound of the lance and the presence of blood and water in the area of the heart. It was the opinion of the team that the Shroud does not contradict the Gospels on any fact and that the Shroud was an authentic archaeological artifact, with many team members believing that the cloth was the actual burial shroud of Jesus Christ.

The scientists were in agreement that the accumulated evidence has shifted the burden of proof to those who believe the Shroud is a forgery.

After many petitions were made to the Vatican for a small piece of the Shroud to be tested by carbon dating, the Vatican relented in 1988 and permitted a seven-centimeter piece to be taken from one of the Shroud's corners. This piece was divided into three parts which were given to three groups of scientists. These were: Professors Paul Damon and Douglas Donahue of Tucson, Wolfli of Zurich, and Professor Hall and Dr. Hedges of Oxford. On October 13 of the same year the results were made known. Carbon dating indicated that the Shroud originated between the years 1260 and 1390. Perplexity and disappointment were keenly felt by Catholics around the world.

Foremost in the minds of many was how someone in the Middle Ages could have produced an image in negative form with its anatomic perfection and complexity.

Many questioned the accuracy of the carbon dating process. Ian Wilson in his *Secret Places, Secret Faces* gives several examples of serious mistakes made by the carbon dating system, and names some scientists who agree with him that the process has not been perfected. In fact, one of the few to admit this was the British Museum laboratory, which revealed that a system error was made in all the datings it issued between 1980 and 1984.

What could have caused an error in calculating the age of the Shroud? First to be considered are the steps taken before the radiocarbon dating is started on a sample. It is pre-treated and cleaned, hopefully of all excess carbon that might have fallen on the sample or might have come in contact with it. But how can porous linen be thoroughly cleaned when the fibers were infiltrated by carbon from the smoke of burning candles and that of incense that was wafted about the Shroud during its many exhibitions? What of the smoke produced from the fire of 1532, when the burned sections of the Shroud produced carbon in the confining space of the silver chest? Another problem is that the sample was taken from an edge of the cloth, where most of the handling had taken place during the many exhibitions. We might also mention that additional carbon could have accumulated from the burning of pollen and threads that were on the cloth during the fire of 1532. During at least six centuries, dust, debris and pollution came in contact with the Shroud and affected the fibers. One wonders if these conditions were taken into account by the carbon dating technicians.

The problem of the Shroud's carbon dating is summarized by Ian Wilson in his *Secret Places, Secret Faces* when he quotes the biblical archaeologist, Dr. Eugenia Nitowski, who advises:

> In any form of inquiry or scientific discipline, it is the weight of evidence which must be considered conclusive. In archaeology, if there are ten lines of evidence, carbon dating being one of them, and it conflicts with the other nine, there is little hesitation to throw out the carbon date as inaccurate.

After all the tests were made by scientific experts, the Shroud remains a mystery. To the faithful, the Shroud is unquestionably the burial cloth of Jesus Christ, a most precious relic which graphically reveals the many sufferings endured by a loving Saviour for our redemption.

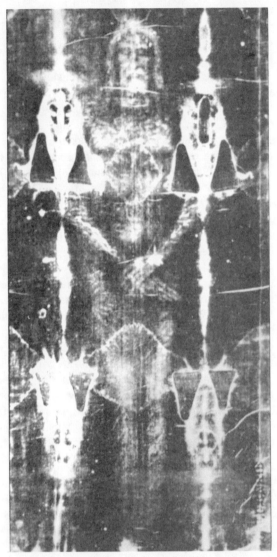

THE HOLY SHROUD of Turin, believed to be the winding sheet in which Christ was buried. The miraculous image imprinted on the cloth shows front and back imprints of the crucified Body of Our Lord. When the cloth was first photographed, in 1898, the image of the Holy Face appeared on the photographic plate. Extensive scientific testing was to follow, yielding the conclusion that the image is indeed miraculous.

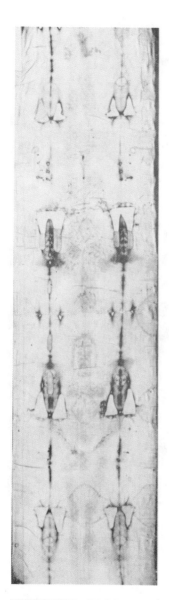

EXHIBITED AT CONSTANTINOPLE for hundreds of years, the Holy Shroud is now enshrined in the Cathedral of San Giovanni Battista in Turin, Italy. The pictures above show negative and positive images of the Shroud.

OUR LORD'S BODY is wrapped in the Shroud in this miniature by G. B. della Rovere.

37

THE VEIL OF VERONICA

Rome, Italy

The veil used by the pious matron, Seraphia, to wipe the face of Jesus as He made His way to Calvary has maintained the same aura of mystery that has intrigued the viewers of the Holy Shroud of Turin. The full-length image of the crucified Christ has attracted a great deal of scientific interest and examination in recent years, but the cloth on which only the face of Jesus is imprinted has been carefully and reverently guarded because of its faded and delicate condition.

It is believed that Seraphia stepped into history during the pause when Simon of Cyrene was recruited to carry the Cross for Jesus, who was then weak with His sufferings. Seraphia's courageous and compassionate act of mercy in wiping the face of Jesus was rewarded when the features of Jesus were miraculously duplicated on the cloth. Known from the earliest times as *vera icon*, Latin for "true image," the words were combined with the passage of time and were gradually applied to Seraphia, thus transforming her name to Veronica.

It is believed that she was about 50 years of age at the time of the incident and that she was a woman of position, being the wife of Sirach, one of the councillors belonging to the Temple.

After Mary Magdalene anointed the head of Jesus she heard His prophetic words as recorded for us in Scripture: "Wherever in the world this gospel is preached, this also that was done shall be told in memory of her." (*Matt.* 26:13). Veronica's compassionate act is not mentioned in Scripture, but she has been memorialized in a different manner since her kindly action is recognized worldwide in the Sixth Station of the Cross.

The veil must have initiated some extraordinary effects, since legend relates that the ailing Tiberius Caesar heard of it and invited Veronica to show it to him. Legend also relates that the Emperor was immediately cured of his grievance after looking upon the wounded face of Jesus.

It is believed that Veronica bequeathed the veil to Clement I, the third successor of St. Peter. During the three centuries of persecution it was kept in the depths of the catacombs and was removed in peaceful times to the church that was built over the tomb of St. Peter. This first church developed into the magnificent Basilica of St. Peter, where the veil is still enshrined.

Protected in a crystal and gilt frame, the veil is kept in a small chapel constructed in one of the four enormous pillars that support the cupola of St. Peter's. In front of this pillar is an heroic-sized statue of Veronica measuring sixteen feet tall, which has been described as one of movement captured in stone. Holding one edge of the veil outward away from her in a sweeping manner, it seems that Veronica was halted between the excitement of her discovery and her eagerness to exhibit her treasure.

A door located at this pillar gives access to two corridors, one leading upward to the small chapel, the other leading downward to the Vatican grottoes. The veil is enshrined inside the second level. The outside of this area which faces the high altar has been adorned by Bernini with balustrades and niches, a magnificent relief and the twisted columns from the ancient church. The keys to the three locks affixed to the vault have been entrusted to the Canons of St. Peter's, who are the guardians of the holy treasure.

The authenticity of the Holy Veil has never been officially doubted. Fr. John van Bolland (1596-1665), whose name was adopted by the Bollandists, the Jesuit editors of the *Acta Sanctorum,* informs us that: "It is the unanimous opinion of all sacred historians and the firm belief of all true Christians that the Veronica *seu Vultus Domini,* now at Rome, is the identical and veritable cloth offered to the Redeemer on His way to Calvary."

St. Bridget, the visionary mystic, reproved anyone who doubted its authenticity, while various Popes have intimated its genuineness by permitting its mention in ancient ceremonials and correspondence as well as its celebration in festivals and processions.

The length of the veil is believed to have originally measured three times its width. This seems to agree with the opinion of the Cathedral of Jaen, Spain which claims to have an exact copy of the face on the veil. This imprinting is believed to have taken place when the veil was folded into three parts, the two contacting sections being miraculously imprinted by its contact with the original. A third portion of the veil is believed to be enshrined somewhere in Milan.

Scheduled expositions of the relic have been varied throughout its history, at times being shown thirteen times a year, at other times only during jubilees or seasons of public calamities. One such exhibition took place during the Papal Jubilee Year of 1350 when pilgrims flocked to Rome, not only to gain the indulgence but also to view the Holy Veil.

An unusual event took place when Pius IX endeavored to appease Heaven and obtain an end to the revolution of 1849 by permitting the Holy Veil to be publicly exposed between the feasts of Christmas and the Epiphany. On the third day of the exposition the face of Our Lord assumed a tinge of color and appeared to be alive, while a soft light surrounded the relic. The face then became more distinct and in relief as it expressed profound severity. The canons of the basilica ordered the immediate pealing of the bells, which attracted crowds of people who witnessed the three-hour manifestation. A document composed by an apostolic notary testifies to the miracle.

After the event, etchings and representations of the effigy were applied to the Holy Face and were then sent to France. This initiated the custom of sending artistic renderings of the veil to Rome to be applied to the original, thus making these copies objects of special devotion. Authenticating seals and stamps testified that they were indeed touched to the original.

Ian Wilson, in his book, *Holy Faces, Secret Places,* tells of a private exhibition that was made in 1950 for the talented Hungarian artist, Isabel Piczek. Several awards were won by this artist, including a competition to create a fresco for the Pontifical Biblical Institute. Specializing in church art, Isabel Piczek came to the attention of high church officials. While visiting St. Peter's one day, a senior cleric within the Vatican brought her into the sacristy and asked her to wait. After nearly an hour he arrived at the sacristy door holding a framed cloth which he said was the Veil of Veronica. Isabel Piczek gives the following description of what she saw:

> On it was a head-sized patch of color, about the same as that on the Holy Shroud, but slightly more brownish...There was a blob of brownish rust color.

It looked almost even, except for some little swirly discolorations...Even with the best imagination you could not make out any face or features, not even the slightest hint of it. The light was not that good and there was glass covering the object. He did not bring it out in apparent fear that people would gather.

From time to time word has surfaced that the veil is indeed terribly faded. It is perhaps for this reason that it is not shown. One investigator who contacted church authorities, asking to study the relic, was told that the veil is in too precarious a condition to be handled for examinations.

In one form or another devotions to the Holy Face have been maintained, but they were greatly encouraged and promoted by the visions and writings of Sister Saint Pierre (d. 1848), a Discalced Carmelite nun of Tours, France. The Archconfraternity of the Holy Face was established and approved by Pope Leo XIII, who encouraged its goals of reparation against blasphemy and the profanation of Sunday. St. Therese of the Child Jesus developed a love for the devotion as a result of this nun's writings and received permission to add to her name that of the Holy Face.

In previous times, and in various locations, a Holy Mass and an Office were celebrated in Veronica's honor with the title of saint being affixed to her name. These liturgical honors were suppressed, however, by St. Charles Borromeo. Neither the early martyrologies nor the present Roman Martyrology mentions her name, but she is still depicted with honor in the Sixth Station of the Cross.

A KINDLY ACT on the part of St. Veronica, wiping Christ's face as He made His way to Calvary, resulted in the miraculous image of the Holy Face.

ARTISTIC REPRESENTATIONS of Veronica's Veil abound, exemplified by Albrecht Dürer's work pictured here.

THE HOLY FACE of Jesus, from the image on Veronica's Veil.

STATUE OF ST. VERONICA. Located in St. Peter's Basilica in Rome, this 16-ft. statue stands before one of four huge pillars facing the altar. (Photo: Art Resource.)

ONE OF THE FOUR MASSIVE PILLARS which support the dome of St. Peter's Basilica. This one is fronted by the enormous statue of St. Veronica. Located inside the pillar at the second level, which is indicated by the two small columns, is the chapel in which the Holy Veil is enshrined.

38

OUR FATHER JESUS THE NAZARENE

(The Black Nazarene)
Quiapo, Manila, The Philippines
1606

In the early years of the Spanish colonization of the Philippines, Quiapo was a marshy place criss-crossed by canals that formed several islets. Named for a water lily locally called Kiapo that thrived in the canals and marshes, the place was principally a fishing village with some areas cultivated for growing crops. As the little village grew, so did a civil government. Eventually, in 1588, Quiapo was designated a parish with St. John the Baptist as its patron. The Reverend Fray Antonio de Nombella was Quiapo's first parish priest. Under his pastoral care the first church of bamboo and nipa was erected. This simple church was unfortunately burned in 1603 by Chinese Revolutionary Suntay. Another church was soon erected to replace it.

At about this time a life-size statue of Our Lord was being crafted by a Mexican artist. The finished statue was entrusted to an unknown Discalced Augustinian Recollect priest who brought it to Manila in the hold of a galleon. It is estimated that the statue arrived in the Philippines about the year 1606.

After its arrival in Manila, the dark skin coloring of the statue became even darker so that it was affectionately known as the Black Nazarene.

About 15 years after its arrival, the Recollect Fathers extensively propagated devotion to the Nazarene and founded on April 20, 1621 a confraternity which was authorized in a Bull signed by Pope Innocent X dated April 20, 1650.

According to the wishes of the Archbishop of Manila, the statue was removed to Quiapo. Although the year is uncertain, it is thought to have arrived a few years before the great fire of 1791 that destroyed the church. Thankfully the statue was rescued, as it was after succeeding structures were destroyed by earthquakes and other fires.

Finally, about the year 1930, a Parish Committee was entrusted with the double responsibility of collecting funds and arranging for the building of a new church with two belfries and a magnificent dome. This is the church that stands today—the church that houses the miraculous image of the Black Nazarene in a niche above the high altar.

Unfortunately, the details of the statue's history have been lost, since the records were destroyed during the liberation of the Philippines during the Second World War. At that time the greater part of Manila was reduced to rubble. Additionally, the records of the Quiapo Church were also destroyed during one of the fires. These lost details matter little to the people, who hold the statue in heartfelt devotion.

Clad in purple robes that are richly embellished with gold embroidery, the life-size statue of the Black Nazarene wears a crown of thorns made of precious metal. Projecting from this crown are three clusters of silver rays which are studded with gems. The figure's semi-kneeling, semi-standing position portrays Our Lord's struggle to rise after falling with the heavy Cross. The figure's face, mouth and eyes manifest the writhing pain Our Lord suffered. It is said that anyone who focuses his eyes on this image of Christ is irresistibly moved to pity.

The Black Nazarene is venerated each year during a week-long celebration which ends dramatically on January 9. On that date the image with the cross is placed on a platform which is pulled by young men holding long ropes. Taken in procession through the streets around the church, the event usually becomes quite energetic since almost everyone struggles to get through the crowd to touch the image. Estimated to number in the thousands, the men who take part are barefoot and wear the traditional attire of the "panata," which consists of rolled-up trousers, a towel around the neck and a white T-shirt printed with the agonized face of the Nazarene. The printing on the shirts reads "Hijos del Nazareno," Sons of the Nazarene. It is said that this might be the only Filipino procession in which women, who usually outnumber men at other religious occasions, are relegated to the background.

To obtain what they ask for, or to express their gratitude for favors received, the devotees of the Black Nazarene have recourse to many forms of devotion. There is a Friday novena which attracts crowds of devotees to the church in Quiapo. As a sign of gratitude, the faithful may vow to walk on their knees from the door of the church to the altar, or make a novena of nine consecutive Fridays in the Quiapo Church, or participate in the procession. They may also wear a purple habit somewhat similar to that of the image. Mothers often dress their children in a purple robe with a yellow cincture to symbolize devotion to the Nazarene.

The Nuestro Padre Jesus Nazareno was blessed by Archbishop Basilio Sancho in the eighteenth century, and by Pope Pius VII in the nineteenth century. Now regarded as part of the city of Manila, the Church of Quiapo was elevated to the dignity of a minor basilica on February 1, 1988 by Pope John Paul II.

Although much of the Nazarene's history is lost, its miraculous reputation has lingered uninterruptedly in the hearts of the Filipino people. This devotion to the Black Nazarene is demonstrated by the many people who reverence the reproductions of the image which are found in almost all the churches of the Philippines.

LIFE-SIZED and dark in color, the statue of Our Father Jesus the Nazarene, or The Black Nazarene, is held in heartfelt devotion by the Philippine people. It is said that anyone who focuses his eyes on this image of Christ is irresistibly moved to pity.

39

OUR LORD IN HIS MISERY

Matrei in Osttirol, Tyrol, Austria
Thirteenth Century

Measuring a little smaller than our state of Maine, Austria is a country whose population is recorded as being between 87% and 90% Roman Catholic. Claiming a sizable section of the majestic Alps, the country is surrounded by seven countries: Germany, Slovakia, Hungary, Yugoslavia, Italy, Switzerland and Liechtenstein. In the secular world the country is known as the home of Mozart and Johann Strauss, among many other musical giants. In the literary field we find Franz Werfel, the author of *The Song of Bernadette*. In the religious world we find shrines of great importance scattered throughout the country, but the western province of Tyrol seems to have been especially blessed.

In the village of Seefeld is the parish church of St. Oswald where a Eucharistic miracle took place. The miraculous host is still kept and exhibited, as are significant indentations in the altar and floor that appeared at the time of the miracle.

In the village of Absam, near Innsbruck, is the church of Our Lady of the Window Pane which enshrines, above the main altar, a pane of glass on which the face of Our Lady was miraculously etched.

What now draws our particular interest to this province and the city of Matrei in Osttirol, a popular tourist center and ski resort, is a miraculous image of Our Lord. Reverenced by Austrians as well as pilgrims from surrounding countries, the Ecce Homo statue of Our Lord encourages both pity and sadness.

The statue traces its origins to the thirteenth century, when it was brought from Jerusalem to Matrei in Osttirol by the knight, Henry of Aufenstein. Miracles of healing that took place soon after its arrival attracted pilgrimages which continue to the present day. A partial list of the many miracles of healing and other favors attributed to devotion to this image is kept in old parish records.

MIRACLES OF HEALING are attributed to the Austrian statue known as Our Lord in His Misery, which dates back to the thirteenth century. The statue pictured here is an exact copy of the original.

40

THE ECCE HOMO OF
ST. TERESA OF AVILA

Avila, Spain
1553

Teresa was prayerful as a child, but her fervor languished during her adolescence due to her fascination with the romantic literature of her day. After a serious illness, however, her devotion was rekindled through the influence of a pious uncle. She became interested in the religious life and entered the Carmelite Convent of the Incarnation in Avila in the year 1536.

Under a relaxed rule, the nuns of this convent were permitted a great deal of socializing and other privileges that were contrary to the original rule. During the first 17 years of her religious life, Teresa tried to enjoy both the delights of prayer and the pleasures of secular conversation. Finally, one day in the year 1553, she had what one writer calls a "shattering experience." The Saint tells us of her experience in Chapter IX of her Autobiography:

> It happened that, entering the oratory one day, I saw an image which had been procured for a certain festival that was observed in the house and had been taken there to be kept for that purpose. It represented Christ sorely wounded; and so conducive was it to devotion that when I looked at it I was deeply moved to see Him thus, so well did it picture what He suffered for us. So great was my distress when I thought how ill I had repaid Him for those wounds that I felt as if my heart were breaking, and I threw myself down beside Him, shedding floods of tears and begging Him to give me strength once for all so that I might not offend Him...I believe I told Him then that I would not rise from that spot until He had granted me what I was beseeching of Him. And I feel sure that this did me

good, for from that time onward I began to improve (in prayer and virtue).

The Saint progressed rapidly in virtue following this experience and she soon began enjoying visions and ecstasies.

Finding the relaxed atmosphere of the convent in opposition to the spirit of prayer for which she felt Our Lord had intended the Order, she began reforming its laxities in 1562 at the cost of countless persecutions and difficulties. Her good friend and advisor, St. John of the Cross, aided her in this endeavor and extended the reform to the friars of the Order.

Under the rigorous interpretation of the rule, she attained the heights of mysticism, enjoyed countless visions and experienced various mystical favors. There seems to be no phenomenon peculiar to the mystical state that she did not experience, yet she remained a shrewd businesswoman, administrator, writer, spiritual counselor and foundress.

Never a healthy woman, the Saint died of her many afflictions on October 4, 1582 at the convent at Alba de Tormes.

Canonized in 1622, she, as well as the Discalced Carmelite Order, was honored when Pope Paul VI officially annexed her name to the list of Doctors of the Church. She is the first woman to join this distinguished group.

The image of the suffering Christ, that proved such an inspiration to the Saint, remains at the Convent of the Incarnation in Avila.

ST. TERESA OF AVILA

ST. TERESA OF AVILA died with this crucifix in her hands.

DEEP PAIN AND COMPASSION filled the soul of St. Teresa of Avila when in 1553 she entered the oratory which contained this devout image. The compelling statue of Christ is preserved to this day.

ORIGINATING THREE CENTURIES AGO, this sculpture of St. Teresa of Avila is kept at the Monastery of the Incarnation in Avila.

41

THE CHI RHO OF CONSTANTINE THE GREAT

Fourth Century

Born between the years 275 and 288, Constantine was the son of a Roman officer, Constantius, who later became Roman Emperor, and St. Helena, who is credited with having found the True Cross.

After serving under Diocletian and later fighting with distinction under Galerius, Constantine was proclaimed Caesar by his troops after the death of his father, Constantius. In Rome, however, Maxentius, who is described as a tyrant and profligate, was also proclaimed Caesar. Five years later, when Maxentius threw down Constantine's statues and attempted to darken his name, Constantine realized that war with Maxentius was inevitable.

Although Constantine's army of between 25,000 and 100,000 men was inferior in number to that of Maxentius, whose army numbered almost 200,000, nevertheless Constantine and his army proudly marched toward Rome to do battle with his rival.

Sometime during the march Constantine had a vision which was recorded for us by both Lactantius and Eusebius. They report that Constantine saw in the sky a cross surrounded by a brilliant, fiery light. Inscribed clearly on the cross were the Latin words, *"In Hoc Signo Vinces"* which mean, "By this sign thou shalt conquer."

Deeply impressed by this vision, Constantine had the standards of his soldiers altered to bear not only a cross, but also a monogram combining the Greek letters X and P, which represent the first and last letters of the name of Christ. This monogram is thought by some to have originated during the vision of Constantine. It is believed this was the first time the letters were used as a symbol of Christ. It should be noted that the majority of the soldiers were pagans, as were many of those who carried the standards.

Strengthened by the vision and surrounded by the symbols of the Saviour, Constantine courageously marched to meet Maxentius and confronted him at the Milvian Bridge that spanned the Tiber

River. Despite the inferior number of his troops, Constantine's army soundly defeated Maxentius, who lost his life in the Tiber on the day of the battle, October 28, of the year 312.

The following year, in gratitude to the God of the Christians, the victor issued the Edict of Milan, in which he extended tolerance to the Christians and encouraged their activities. Previous to the edict Christians had suffered bloody persecution. Caesars that followed Constantine made Christianity the state religion.

In Rome, the monogram of Christ, an X and P, was placed in the hand of a statue of Constantine. The pedestal of this statue bore the inscription: "By the aid of this salutary token of strength I have freed my city from the yoke of tyranny and restored to the Roman Senate and People the ancient splendour and glory."

It is believed that St. Helena embraced Christianity soon after the battle, having been influenced, no doubt, by her son's vision and its prophetic outcome.

For his part, Constantine resisted conversion and was baptized only when he felt the approach of death. After suffering from an undisclosed illness, he died in May of 337, wearing, it is said, the white robe of a neophyte.

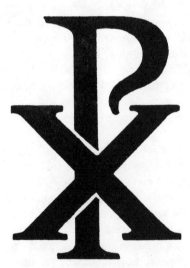

Above: THE CHI RHO.
Opposite: CONSTANTINE'S VISION in the sky included the words, *"In Hoc Signo Vinces"* ("By this sign thou shalt conquer"). He and his army were thus spurred on to victory over the cruel Maxentius and his many troops.

42

PORTRAIT OF THE DIVINE MERCY

Lagiewniki, Krakow, Poland
1931

Helen Kowalska (1905-1938), the recipient of the visions which resulted in the miraculous image of the Divine Mercy, was born in the village of Glogowiec, Poland, the third of ten children. After receiving a proper Catholic education she began to work at the age of 16 as a servant in various households to financially help her parents. Four years later, she received the name Sister Mary Faustina when she entered the Congregation of the Sisters of Our Lady of Mercy, an order dedicated to the rehabilitation of wayward women and the care of girls in need of protection. Although suffering intermittently throughout her life from various ailments, she nevertheless served her community well, while rapidly advancing in virtue.

After six years of religious life and a number of communications from Our Lord, Sr. Faustina received an extraordinary vision on February 22, 1931, that would result in the devotion known as the Divine Mercy. On the advice of her confessor and her Mother Superior, she began to write a detailed account of her spiritual life. This diary, known as *Divine Mercy in My Soul,* was written in six notebooks, the first of which gives details concerning the vision. Sr. Faustina describes the event in this manner:

> In the evening, when I was in my cell, I saw the Lord Jesus clothed in a white garment. One hand was raised in the gesture of blessing, the other was touching the garment at the breast. From beneath the garment, slightly drawn aside at the breast, there were emanating two large rays, one red, the other pale. In silence I kept my gaze fixed on the Lord; my soul was struck with awe, but also with great joy. After a while, Jesus said to me, "Paint an image according to the pattern you see, with the signature: Jesus, I trust in You (Jezu, Ufam

Tobie). I desire that this image be venerated, first in your chapel, and then throughout the world. I promise that the soul that will venerate this image will not perish. I also promise victory over its enemies already here on earth, especially at the hour of death. I Myself will defend it as My own glory."

Our Lord added, "Let the sinner not be afraid to approach Me. The flames of mercy are burning Me, clamoring to be spent; I want to pour them out upon souls."

Sr. Faustina experienced a number of difficulties and delays in arranging for the painting of the portrait, but finally, in 1934, with the permission of her confessor and Mother Superior, an artist was selected. Although Eugene Kazimierowski endeavored with great care to paint the portrait according to Sr. Faustina's instructions, which she personally gave him, she was deeply disappointed when she saw the finished work since it did not convey the splendor she had seen. Later she complained to Our Lord, "Who will paint You as beautiful as You are?" She then heard these words: "Not in the beauty of the color, nor of the brush lies the greatness of this image, but in My grace." Later Our Lord added, "My gaze from this image is like My gaze from the Cross."

Sr. Faustina's confessor inquired about the two rays and told the Sister to ask Our Lord to explain their meaning. During prayer the holy religious heard these words:

"The two rays denote Blood and Water. The pale ray stands for the Water, which makes souls righteous. The red ray stands for the Blood, which is the life of souls. . .

"These two rays issued forth from the very depths of My tender mercy when My agonized heart was opened by a lance on the Cross.

"These rays shield souls from the wrath of My Father. Happy is the one who will dwell in their shelter, for the just hand of God shall not lay hold of him. . . ."

Our Lord once told Sr. Faustina, "I am offering people a vessel with which they are to keep coming for graces to the fountain of mercy. That vessel is this Image with the signature: 'Jesus, I trust in You.'"

In addition to the portrait, Our Lord also requested the establishment of a Feast of Mercy. In Sr. Faustina's diary there are at least fourteen messages of Our Lord regarding the feast, one of which reads: "I want this image...to be solemnly blessed on the first Sunday after Easter; that Sunday is to be the Feast of Mercy."

Elsewhere Our Lord states: "...Whoever approaches the Fount of Life on this day will be granted complete remission of sins and punishment." Sometime later Our Lord further clarified the requirements to be performed in order to obtain this privilege: "...The soul that will go to Confession and receive Holy Communion shall obtain complete forgiveness of sins and punishment." Confession can, of course, be made a few days before the feast.

Our Lord also requested the observance of the Hour of Mercy. He explained it in these words:

> "At three o'clock, implore My mercy, expecially for sinners; and, if only for a brief moment, immerse yourself in My Passion, particularly in My abandonment at the moment of agony. This is the hour of great mercy for the whole world...In this hour I will refuse nothing to the soul that makes a request of Me in virtue of My Passion."

There is also a Chaplet of Mercy whose arrangement and prayers were specified by Our Lord Himself. One morning in the chapel, Sr. Faustina heard these words:

> "First of all, you will say one Our Father and Hail Mary and the I Believe in God. Then on the Our Father beads of the Rosary, you will say the following words: 'Eternal Father, I offer You the Body and Blood, Soul and divinity of Your dearly beloved Son, Our Lord Jesus Christ, in atonement for our sins and those of the whole world.' On the Hail Mary beads you will say the following words: 'For the sake of His sorrowful Passion have mercy on us and on the whole world.' In conclusion, three times you will recite these words: 'Holy God, Holy Mighty One, Holy Immortal One, have mercy on us and on the whole world.'"

The Lord requested that this chaplet be recited for nine days before the Feast of Mercy, beginning on Good Friday. "By this novena, I will grant every possible grace to souls."

Our Lord also promised:

> "Whoever will recite it (the chaplet) will receive great mercy at the hour of death. Priests will recommend it to sinners as their last hope of salvation. Even if there were a sinner most hardened, if he were to recite this chaplet only once, he would receive grace from My infinite mercy. I desire that the whole world know My infinite mercy. I desire to grant unimaginable graces to those souls who trust in My mercy."

So anxious is Our Lord to impart His mercy that, in addition to the picture, the chaplet and the special graces given on the Feast of Mercy, He also gave a special prayer, which reads, "O Blood and Water, which gushed forth from the Heart of Jesus as a fount of Mercy for us, I trust in You." Our Lord promised, "When you say this prayer with a contrite heart and with faith on behalf of some sinner, I will give him the grace of conversion."

Our Lord also recommended that this prayer be used in a novena for the Holy Father's intentions. "It should consist of thirty-three acts; that is, repetition of the short prayer which I have taught you to the Divine Mercy."

*   *   *

Sr. Faustina died of multiple tuberculosis on October 5, 1938, at the age of 33 at the convent of the Congregation of the Sisters of Our Lady of Mercy in Lagiewniki, Krakow. First buried in the convent cemetery, Sr. Faustina's remains were later transferred to a tomb in the sisters' chapel.

Of special interest in this same chapel, is an image of the Divine Mercy which is found above a side altar. Painted by the artist Adolph Hyla in 1943, five years after Sr. Faustina's death, it was the artist's votive offering to the sisters in thanksgiving for his family's preservation during World War II. Although all images of the Divine Mercy possess an exceptional quality according to Our Lord's words which are quoted above, it is this portrait, found in the sisters' chapel, which "is renowned for countless graces."

Just as Sr. Faustina had prophesied, the Devotion to the Divine Mercy spread rapidly and became known even during her lifetime. Another of Sr. Faustina's prophecies was fulfilled when in 1958 the devotion was prohibited by Church authorities. Since the introduction of the devotion seemed premature by some Church authorities, the suspension was deemed appropriate to give them time to further examine the many facets of the devotion and to obtain many original documents that were previously unavailable.

During the 20-year suspension, one prelate's faith in Sr. Faustina and her revelations never faltered. He was Archbishop Karol Wojtyla, who began in 1965 the solemn Informative Process relating to the life and virtues of Sr. Faustina. Two years later, after Karol Cardinal Wojtyla closed the solemn session, the Process was sent to Rome to the Sacred Congregation for the Causes of Saints.

Suspension of the devotion was lifted by the Sacred Congregation for the Doctrine of the Faith on April 15, 1978. Six months later, Karol Cardinal Wojtyla became Pope John Paul II. On April 18, 1993, he beatified Sr. Faustina and affixed the title "Blessed" to her name.

*   *   *

Our Lord once told Blessed Faustina these words of consolation for His beloved children, which we should seriously consider:

> "Souls who spread the honor of My mercy I shield through their entire lives as a tender mother her infant, and at the hour of death I will not be a Judge for them, but the Merciful Saviour. At that last hour, a soul has nothing with which to defend itself except My mercy. Happy is the soul that during its lifetime immersed itself in the Fountain of Mercy, because justice will have no hold on it."

Further information about the devotion to the Divine Mercy and prayers to be said during the novena of chaplets can be obtained from a booklet published by the Marians of the Immaculate Conception, Marian Helpers, Stockbridge, MA 01263.

THE DIVINE MERCY painting located in the chapel of the Congregation of the Sisters of Our Lady of Mercy in Lagiewniki, Krakow, Poland.

— SELECTED BIBLIOGRAPHY —

Allardyce, Isabel. *Historic Shrines of Spain.* Franciscan Missionary Press. Quebec, Canada. 1912.

Auclair, Marcelle. *Teresa of Avila.* Doubleday & Company, Inc. Garden City, New York. 1961.

Ball, Ann. *Holy Names of Jesus.* Our Sunday Visitor, Inc. Huntington, Indiana. 1990.

Bardi, Mons. Giuseppe. *St. Gemma Galgani.* St. Paul Editions. Boston, Massachusetts. 1951.

Brewer, E. Cobham. *A Dictionary of Miracles.* Cassell & Company. New York. 1884.

Brown, Raphael, Translator. *The Little Flowers of St. Francis.* Doubleday & Company, Inc. Garden City, New York. 1958.

Chiesa Santuario di S. Maria Maddalena. The Church of St. Mary Magdalene. Rome, Italy.

Cioni, Raffaello. *S. Veronica Giuliani.* Monastero Delle Cappuccine. Citta Di Castello, Italy. 1964.

Colette de Corbie. Monastere de Ste. Claire. Poligny, France.

Collected Works of St. John of the Cross. Translated by Kieran Kavanaugh, O.C.D. and Otilio Rodriguez, O.C.D. Institute of Carmelite Studies. Washington, D.C. 1973.

Corcoran, O.S.A., Rev. M. J. *Our Own St. Rita.* Benziger Brothers. New York. 1919.

Cruz, Joan Carroll. *Relics.* Our Sunday Visitor, Inc. Huntington, Indiana. 1984.

. . . *The Incorruptibles.* TAN Books and Publishers, Inc. Rockford, Illinois. 1977.

Gianan, Rev. Francisco S. *Brief History of the Black Nazarene and Quiapo Church.* Minor Basilica of the Black Nazarene.

Heller, Dr. John H. *Report on the Shroud of Turin.* Houghton Mifflin. Boston. 1983.

Histoire et Legende de Déols. Église de Déols. Déols, France.

Holy Bible, Douay-Rheims Version. TAN Books and Publishers, Inc. Rockford, Illinois. 1989.

Holy Infant of Good Health. Morelia, Mexico. 1956.

Johnston, Francis. *The Wonder of Guadalupe.* TAN Books and Publishers, Inc. Rockford, Illinois. 1981.

Kavanaugh, O.C.D., Kieran and Otilio Rodriguez, O.C.D. Translators. *The Collected Works of St. John of the Cross.* Institute of Carmelite Studies. Washington, D.C. 1973.

Keyes, Frances Parkinson. *Three Ways of Love.* Hawthorn Books, Inc. New York. 1963.

Kowalska, Sr. M. Faustina, *Divine Mercy in My Soul—The Diary of Sr. M. Faustina Kowalska.* Marian Press, Stockbridge, Massachusetts. 1987.

Lazzarini, Sac. Pietro. *Volto Santo di Lucca.* Societa Editrice Internazionale. Torino, Italy. 1952.

Lopez de Lara, J. Jesus. *El Nino de Santa Maria de Atocha.* Santuario de Plateros. Fresnillo, Mexico. 1992.

A Lover of the Cross—St. Gemma Galgani. Passionista Monastery of St. Gemma Galgani. Lucca, Italy. 1940.

Michalenko, Mic, Fr. Seraphim and Vinny Flynn. *The Divine Mercy Message and Devotions.* Marian Helpers,

234

Stockbridge, Massachusetts. 1993.

Monastery of the Incarnation in Avila. Monasterio de la Encarnacion. Avila, Spain. 1978.

Mother Mary Francis. *Walled in Light, Saint Colette.* Franciscan Herald Press. Chicago. 1959.

My Personal Devotion to the Holy Infant Jesus and the Blessed Virgin Mary. The Rosarian Dominican Sisters. Silverado, California.

Nemec, Ludvik. *The Infant of Prague.* Benziger Brothers, Inc. New York. 1958.

Parente, Pascal P. *A City on a Mountain, Padre Pio of Pietrelcina.* A Grail Publication. St. Meinrad's Abbey. 1952.

Piadosa Leyenda del Senor Del Veneno. Catedral Metropolitana de Mexico.

Pius of the Name of Mary, Fr. *The Life of Saint Paul of the Cross.* P. O'Shea. New York. 1924.

Rahm, S.J., Harold. *Am I Not Here.* AMI Press. Washington, New Jersey. 1962.

Raymond of Capua, Bl. *Life of Saint Catherine of Siena.* P. J. Kenedy & Sons. New York. 1853.

Romanelli, Emanuele. *Santa Maria in Aracoeli.* Rome, Italy.

Ruffin, C. Bernard. *Padre Pio: The True Story.* Our Sunday Visitor, Inc. Huntington, Indiana. 1982.

Sanctuary of Our Mother of Good Counsel. Sanctuario Madonna del Buon Consiglio. Genazzano, Italy.

Santo Nino Church and Monastery. An Augustinian Legacy to the Filipino People. Augustinian Fathers. Basilica del Santo Nino. Cebu, The Philippines.

Senor de los Milagros de Buga. Basilica del Sr. delos Milagros. Buga, Colombia.

Sicardo, O.S.A., Fr. Joseph. *St. Rita of Cascia, Saint of the Impossible.* TAN Books and Publishers, Inc. Rockford, Illinois. 1990.

St. Teresa of Avila. *The Autobiography of St. Teresa of Avila.* Doubleday & Co., Inc. Garden City, New York. 1960.

Stevenson, Kenneth E. and Gary R. Habermas. *Verdict on the Shroud.* Servant Books. Ann Arbor, Michigan. 1981.

Vann, O.P., Gerald. *Saint Thomas Aquinas.* Benziger Brothers, Inc. New York. 1947.

Von Kleist, S.T.D., Rev. Baron. *The Wonderful Crucifix of Limpias, Remarkable Manifestations.* Benziger Brothers. New York. 1922.

Wilcox, Robert K. *Shroud.* Macmillan Publishing Co., Inc. New York. 1977.

Wilson, Ian. *Holy Faces, Secret Places.* Doubleday. Garden City, N.Y. 1991.
. . . *The Mysterious Shroud.* Doubleday. Garden City, N.Y. 1986.

True stories of 100 beloved Marian images...

MIRACULOUS IMAGES
OF OUR LADY

No. 1222. 441 Pages.
32-page Color Section.
PB. Impr. ISBN 4844.

20.00

(Price Guaranteed
thru 12/31/96)

by Joan Carroll Cruz

Best-selling writer Joan Carroll Cruz—author of *Prayers and Heavenly Promises, The Incorruptibles, Secular Saints, Eucharistic Miracles*—has done her best work yet in *Miraculous Images of Our Lady.* For here are 100 true stories of Church-approved miraculous statues, paintings and other images of Our Lady from all parts of the globe and spanning almost 2,000 years. Included are images that have spoken, that have brought miraculous cures and other special favors, that have helped in the construction of Catholic churches, that have shed luminous rays leading to their discovery in hidden places, that have given off a celestial fragrance, or that have suddenly and unexplainedly become extremely heavy so as to resist being moved from a favored place. Also described are images of Our Lady weeping blood and tears, of Our Lady lovingly holding the Infant Jesus, as well as the ornate and costly garments the faithful have created for these dear figures, plus the special feastdays celebrated in their honor.

Ranging across Italy, France, the U.S., Japan, Mexico, etc., the stories shared by Mrs. Cruz tell of the images of Our Lady of Guadalupe, Akita, Pompeii, Prompt Succor (New Orleans), Our Lady of the Smile (through which St. Therese the Little Flower was cured at age 10), Our Lady of the Holy Rosary, The Comforter of the Afflicted, The Madonna of Consolation, Mother of Divine Love, Our Lady of Zapopan (Mexico) and many, many more! Scores of pictures make the book come alive. This is a perfect book for the entire family and a great treasure for your home library!

At your Bookdealer or direct from the Publisher.

U.S. & CAN. POST/HDLG.: If total order = $1-$5, add $1.50; $5.01-$10, add $3; $10.01-$30.00, add $4; $30.01-$50, add $5; $50.01-up, add $6.

TAN BOOKS AND PUBLISHERS, INC.
P.O. Box 424, Rockford, Illinois 61105

If you have enjoyed this book, consider making your next selection from among the following . . .

Prices guaranteed through June 30, 1996.

At your Bookdealer or direct from the Publisher.

Prices guaranteed through June 30, 1996.

ABOUT THE AUTHOR

Joan Carroll Cruz is a native of New Orleans and was educated by the School Sisters of Notre Dame. She attended grade school, high school and college under their tutelage. About her teachers Mrs. Cruz says, "I am especially indebted to the sisters who taught me for five years at the boarding school at St. Mary of the Pines in Chatawa, Mississippi. I cannot thank them enough for their dedication, their fine example and their religious fervor, which made such an impression on me." Mrs. Cruz has been a tertiary in the Discalced Carmelite Secular Order (Third Order) for the past 25 years. She is married to Louis Cruz, who owns a swimming pool repair and maintenance business. They are the parents of five children.

Other books by Mrs. Cruz include *Miraculous Images of Our Lady, Prayers and Heavenly Promises, Secular Saints, The Incorruptibles* and *Eucharistic Miracles,* all published by TAN Books and Publishers, Inc.; *The Desires of Thy Heart,* a novel with a strong Catholic theme published in hardcover by Tandem Press in 1977 and in paperback by Signet with an initial printing of 600,000 copies; and *Relics,* published by Our Sunday Visitor, Inc. For her non-fiction books Mrs. Cruz depends heavily on information received from foreign shrines, churches, convents and monasteries. The material she receives requires the services of several translators. Mrs. Cruz is currently working on another book which also involves a great deal of research.